Chess *and the* Art of War

Chess *and the* Art of War

Ancient wisdom to make you a better player

Al Lawrence

International Grandmaster
Elshan Moradiabadi

CHARTWELL
BOOKS

A QUARTO BOOK

This edition published in 2016 by
CHARTWELL BOOKS
an imprint of Book Sales
a division of
Quarto Publishing Group USA Inc.
142 West 36th Street, 4th Floor
New York, New York 10018
USA

ISBN: 978-0-7858-3281-2

Conceived, designed,
and produced by
Quarto Publishing plc
The Old Brewery
6 Blundell Street
London N7 9BH

Senior editor: Claire Waite Brown
Art director: Caroline Guest
Copy editor and proofreader:
    Ian Kingston
Designer: Hugh Schermuly
Picture researcher: Sarah Bell
Editorial assistant: Georgia Cherry
Indexer: Diana LeCore
Creative director: Moira Clinch
Publisher: Paul Carslake

Printed in China
by 1010 Printing International Ltd

Contents

Chess and war

"Chess is war over the board," Bobby Fischer famously said. Many consider Fischer the greatest chess mind who ever pushed a pawn.

Indeed, chess has its origin in war and is thus combat made civil. Around the 6th century, the game *chaturanga* developed in the Gupta Empire—in an area we now know as northern India. The game pieces were based on the elements of actual battle units of the then-existing armies. From there, *chaturanga* was exported to Persia. (Co-author and International Grandmaster Elshan Moradiabadi boasts an ancient chess pedigree.) The game morphed slowly into chess and spread across medieval Europe. About the time of its final rule changes, the modern game of chess sailed to the New World with the explorers of the 15th and 16th centuries. Nowadays there isn't a corner of the Earth where chess isn't played.

The Art of War is the most influential book ever written on how to conduct an army in battle. Written thousands of years ago, it continues to be required reading for modern military leaders around the world, and influential business tycoons have also mandated its study. Successful politicians, stock traders, and sports coaches have all employed and recommended its timeless wisdom.

We know the man who wrote these famous 13 chapters by his honorific title of Sun Tzu. Most scholars accept that he was an actual flesh-and-blood general named Sun Wu who, around 500 BCE, commanded victorious armies for a span of some 20 years. His followers continued to make use of his strategies. Despite the mists of 2,500 years of history, we can be certain that *The Art of War* is indeed an ancient treatise, since, in 1972, construction workers in the Chinese city of Linyi in the Shandong province accidentally unearthed an ancient tomb dating from the 2nd century BCE. Among the treasures were bamboo slips recording *The Art of War*.

Chess-generalship and military training have been linked since the game's beginnings. To this day, modern military researchers continue to use chess, as they do *The Art of War*, as a training tool and a model of military thinking.

We need to point out that, unlike war, chess offers benefits to humankind. Chess improves concentration, logical and critical thinking, persistence, memory, patience, self-confidence, self-control, and sportsmanship. It does this for children and adults.

So one of the best uses we can make of *The Art of War* is to learn to play better chess by applying Sun Tzu's memorable military wisdom. We're sure he'd like the idea.

Al Lawrence
Elshan Moradiabadi
Texas Tech University, Lubbock, Texas

66 He will win who, prepared himself, waits to take the enemy unprepared. 99

Sun Tzu dwells again and again on preparing for battle—organizing your line troops, readying your lieutenants, and, most of all, preparing yourself as the ultimate commander. A major part of preparing to lead any army is studying famous battles of the past.

This section will give you the skills to study chess games ancient and modern. As a West Point cadet studies the ploys of Alexander the Great, Caesar and General George S. Patton, you will be able to recreate the stratagems of Paul Morphy, Bobby Fischer, and Magnus Carlsen. To adapt a well-known maxim, "He who fails to study the chess mistakes of the past is doomed to repeat them."

Reading and writing chess

Chess players around the world use a universal system, called *notation*, to record games. Knowing notation is the key that unlocks the treasure trove of chess brilliancies. It also gives you a way to record and analyze your own game—another key step in playing better chess.

The vertical columns of squares running up and down the board are called *files* and are lettered from "a" to "h." The horizontal rows of squares that run sideways are called *ranks* and are numbered from "1" to "8."

An individual square gets its name from the file and rank that cross through it. Let's look at a board that gives the "address" of every square. The address of the highlighted square below is "e4."

	a	b	c	d	e	f	g	h
8	a8	b8	c8	d8	e8	f8	g8	h8
7	a7	b7	c7	d7	e7	f7	g7	h7
6	a6	b6	c6	d6	e6	f6	g6	h6
5	a5	b5	c5	d5	e5	f5	g5	h5
4	a4	b4	c4	d4	**e4**	f4	g4	h4
3	a3	b3	c3	d3	e3	f3	g3	h3
2	a2	b2	c2	d2	e2	f2	g2	h2
1	a1	b1	c1	d1	e1	f1	g1	h1

Every square on the chessboard has an address. Here the e4 square is highlighted.

To make writing and reading chess fast and easy, each piece except the pawn is assigned a single letter. The symbols right are used to represent the pieces on diagrams of the chessboard. In English, we use these abbreviations:

King = K   Knight = N

Queen = Q   Rook = R

Bishop = B   Pawn = the file it's on

We number each set of white and black moves. The move pair

1. e4 d5

means that on the first move of the game, White pushed the pawn in front of the king (the e-pawn) forward two squares. Black pushed the pawn in front of the queen (the d-pawn) two squares. Notice that only the arrival square is given in each case. We don't need to say which square the pawn moved from, because only one pawn could possibly move to e4 (or d5) in this position.

Captures are indicated by "x." So …

2. exd5 Qxd5

shows us that White captured Black's pawn on d5, and that Black recaptured with the queen. The position now looks like this:

3. Nc3 Qa5

Now the position on the board is this:

You will notice that the moves are listed in bold type. It is conventional to use bold to distinguish the moves of a game from comments or alternative lines of play.

Other symbols you will come across in this and other chess books are:

+ Check
# Checkmate
= Promotion
… Indicates that the next move is by Black
e.p. *En passant*
0-0 Kingside castling
0-0-0 Queenside castling
!! An excellent move
! A good move
? A weak move
?? A blunder

KEY

In this book we use the following symbols where relevant on the board diagrams:

direction

capture

indicates when a piece is fenced in

66 By method and discipline are to be understood the marshaling of the army in its proper subdivisions, the graduations of rank among the officers, the maintenance of roads by which supplies may reach the army, and the control of military expenditure. **99**

Chapter 1

The battlefield and the armies

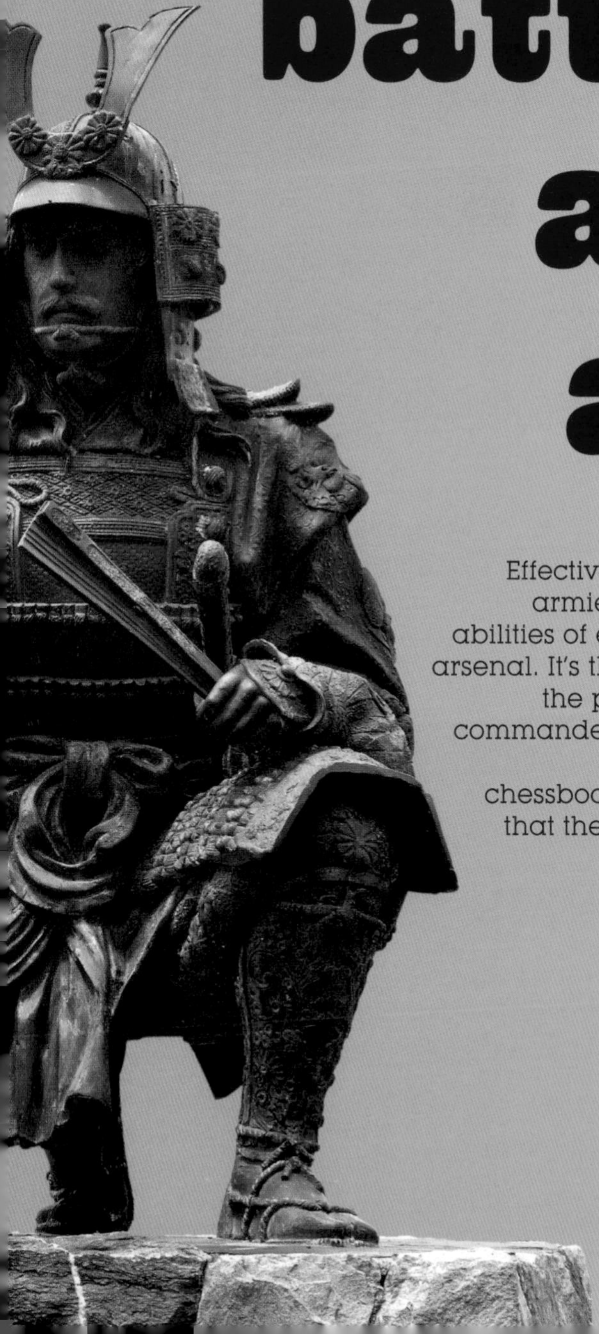

Effective commanders must know every aspect of their armies. They should have a complete mastery of the abilities of every kind of soldier and every weapon in their arsenal. It's the same in chess. A good player needs to know the powers and limitations of all the pieces. Military commanders must also know how to deploy their troops in many different types of terrain. Fortunately, the chessboard battlefield is always the same—but we'll see that the position of the pawns can make a game seem like a downhill attack or trench warfare.

66 If you know the enemy and know yourself, you need not fear the results of a hundred battles. 99

A military commander from any era needed to know the strength and capabilities of his opponent's army. That information is called intelligence—"intel" for short, a word you hear in many a spy movie. Sun Tzu dedicates one of his seven chapters to this topic. It's true that, in chess, both sides know exactly what assets the other general begins with, but the winner is usually the one who understands all the army's capabilities better.

How the pieces move

Chess is a battle between two armies, called White and Black, that begin the contest as equals. White always gets to make the first move. Then the two sides take turns. The battlefield is the chessboard.

♖ The rook

The rook's name goes back to the Persian *rokh*, meaning tower or castle. But don't give yourself away as a novice by calling a rook a "castle."

Each player has two rooks and their movement is easy to master. Think of the rook as a tank that can charge straight ahead or in reverse, or turn left or right. On an empty board, the rook can move in a straight line in one direction as many squares as its general desires.

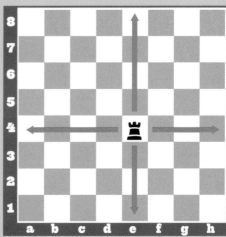

The rook can move along files and ranks.

Note that the board is always set up with a light square on the right of each player. Chess players say, "Light on right!"

There are 32 chessmen on the board at the beginning of a battle, 16 on each side. But there are only six kinds of chessmen—in Sun Tzu's terms, six "subdivisions": rooks, kings, queens, bishops, knights, and pawns.

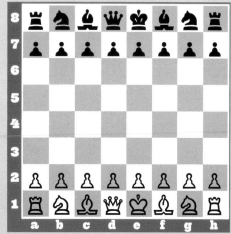

The chessmen set up to begin a game. In chess literature, White moves "up" the board.

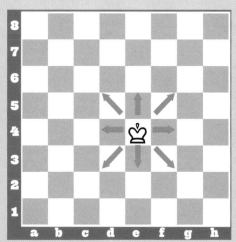 The king

His highness can move one square in any direction as long as he is not under attack (check) from an enemy piece. Of course, each side has only one king!

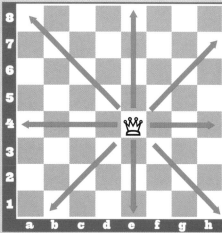 The queen

The most powerful piece on the chessboard, the queen moves like the king, but much more so. On an empty board, she can move in any one direction as many squares as she wants.

The king takes only one royal step (square) at a time.

The queen is the most powerful chess piece. She can move as any other piece except the knight.

The bishop

Your two bishops move on differently colored squares. Bishops move only on the diagonals. Each of your bishops can cover only the light or dark squares.

The knight

The knight can jump over friends and foes alike. Its move adds magic to the game of chess. Most often, its move is described as an "L."

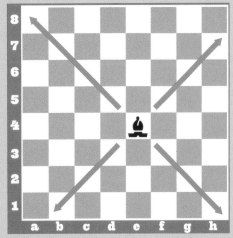

A bishop that begins on a light square can never land on a dark square.

The knight can jump over pieces. It always lands on an alternate-color square.

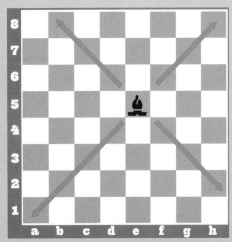

A bishop that begins on a dark square can never land on a light square!

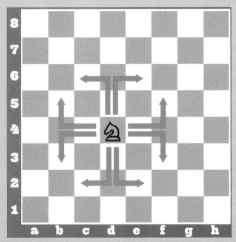

The knight's move is often described as an "L"-shape.

The pawn

The eight pawns in each chess army represent the infantry, the most numerous and least powerful chessmen. (Technically, pawns are not called pieces.) As foot soldiers have in every war throughout time, they stand in front of their officers, ready to walk only straight ahead into battle. As in real combat, they are almost always the first casualties.

On the first move, a pawn can advance either one square or two. After that, it moves one square at a time.

Unlike the pieces, pawns can never move backward.

Capturing

All the chess pieces, but not the pawns, capture as they move. When they can land on an enemy piece, they can remove that piece from the board. But you are not required to take an enemy piece unless it's your only legal move.

Pawns, however, capture differently than they move. Imagine a pawn holding a spear at an angle to his body. That's how the chess foot soldier captures, on the diagonal. It can't capture straight ahead. We suppose his shield is in the way.

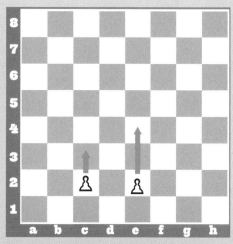

The pawn can leap two squares into the battle on its first move. After that, it's one square at a time and always straight ahead.

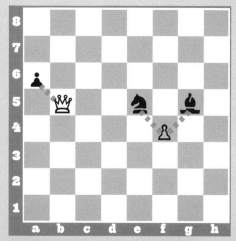

If White is to move, his pawn can capture the black knight or bishop. If Black is to move, his pawn can capture the white queen.

> **66 While heeding the profit of my counsel, avail yourself also of any helpful circumstances over and beyond the ordinary rules. 99**

An inexperienced commander is often at a disadvantage in the field because he knows only the basics. You'll find many casual chess players who don't know all three of these special rules, but they're critical to good play.

Three special moves

The rules of chess are standardized around the world. Don't let anyone tell you differently. There are no "optional" rules. But there are three very important rules that many players don't know or aren't really sure about.

Promotion

If a lowly pawn makes it all the way to the other side of the board, it may be promoted to any piece (of its own color) other than a king. In military terms, it's a way of both rewarding a gallant charger and of gaining reinforcements. Almost always, such a pawn is promoted to a powerful queen. Yes, you can have more than one queen, several rooks, bishops, or knights on the board at the same time if you're successful in promoting that many pawns!

The value of the pieces

Playing chess involves trading pieces and pawns, so to play intelligently you have to know the relative value of the pieces. You will find some occasions on which you decide to "sacrifice" a piece for a less valuable one. The king can't be traded and must be protected, so it is infinitely valuable.

♛ = 9 points

♜ = 5 points

♝ = 3 points

♞ = 3 points

♟ = 1 point

Use this scale as a general guide—for example, exchanging a rook for a bishop and two pawns may be roughly an even trade. The queens and rooks are referred to as major pieces, and the bishops and knights as minor pieces.

Castling

Castling is a key move that whisks your king into safety and away from the dangerous center of the board, while it brings one of your rooks into the game. Castling is the only move that lets a player move two pieces at once. Castling is played by both players in nearly every master game.

In castling the king moves two squares to the left or right from its original square and toward one of his rooks. The rook lands on the square on the other side of the king. In most games, a player castles kingside, toward the rook that the king is closest to. The notation for kingside castling is "0-0." When a player castles queenside, the king moves toward the farthest away rook. The notation for queenside castling is "0-0-0."

There are four important prerequisites to castling.

- Neither the king nor the rook involved may have moved previously. (Hence a player can castle only once in a game.)
- No chess piece of either color can stand between the king and rook.
- A king can't castle out of check or checkmate (see pages 18–21).
- While castling, the king cannot cross any square controlled by the enemy.

En passant

Likely the least understood chess rule, *en passant* is French for "in passing." This rule applies only when a pawn uses the option to advance two squares on its first move and there is an enemy pawn that could have taken it had it advanced only one square. But a player must exercise the right to use *en passant* as soon as it's possible. If you wait even one move, you lose the option.

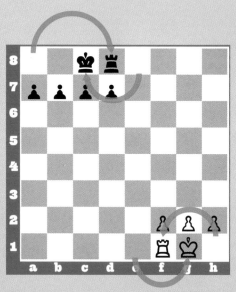

White has castled kingside (0-0). Black has castled queenside 0-0-0.)

White's pawn can advance to d4 but can't avoid capture. Black could then capture it as though it had moved to d3.

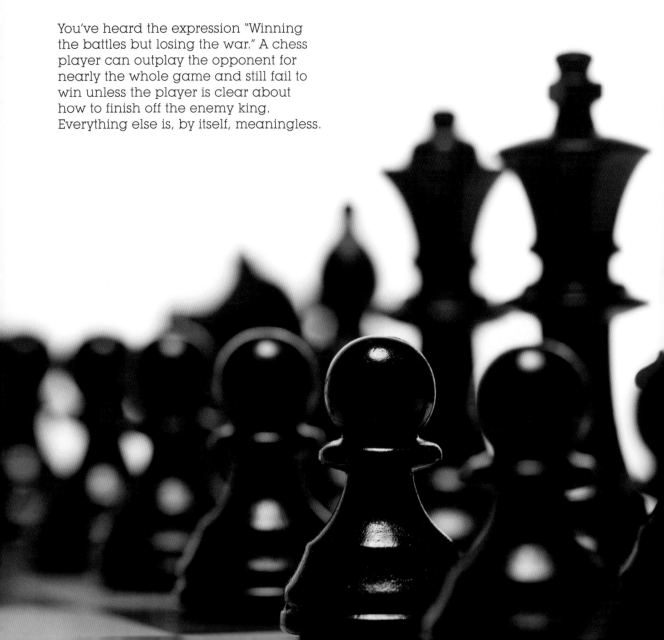

66 The value of a whole army—a mighty host of a million men—is dependent on one man alone. 99

You've heard the expression "Winning the battles but losing the war." A chess player can outplay the opponent for nearly the whole game and still fail to win unless the player is clear about how to finish off the enemy king. Everything else is, by itself, meaningless.

Checkmate: the goal of chess

The goal of chess is to checkmate your opponent's king—to attack him so that he can't escape from the attack. That's how you win. Checkmate ends the game.

Here's a classic checkmate pattern that teaches us a lot about chess. The white rook attacks the black king—this is called *giving check* (explained in more detail later). Any piece or pawn, other than the king, can give check. If the black king can't escape check, it's checkmate. Here he can't because the white king hems his rival in, keeping him on the rim of the board. That's because a king can't move into check, even from another king.

Here's another simple checkmate that some players call "the queen sandwich." Once again the imprisoned King is placed in check, this time by the enemy queen. The white king can't capture the queen because she's protected by her king.

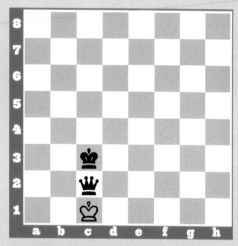

Black has checkmated White.

Does it always take at least two pieces to checkmate? Look at this example. The position above is an example of back-rank mate, which occurs often in amateur games. The black king is hemmed in by his own pawns. (Pawns can't move backward!) He can't escape check.

White has checkmated Black.

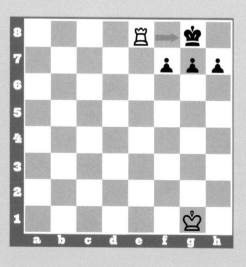

White has checkmated Black with only a rook.

66 Ponder and deliberate before you make a move. 99

More than 100 years ago, a regiment in the Mexican–American war was credited with "snatching victory from the jaws of defeat." That's possible in chess. But it's also possible to "snatch a draw from the jaws of defeat," and even, to a player's terrible regret, to "snatch defeat from the jaws of victory." So ponder your moves carefully indeed.

Check and stalemate

Now we look at two kinds of special moves that are not checkmate.

Check

A simple check attacks the king. The player giving check to his opponent has the right to say "check" quietly—but not with a dramatic threat, as portrayed in many movies. In serious games, most experienced players do not say "check."

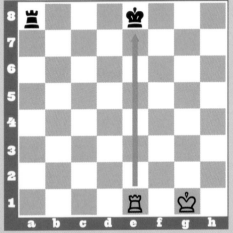

White's rook checks the black king down the e-file. Black can simply move the king and have an equal game.

The threatened king can't delay. He must immediately get out of check. He has three ways to do this.

- The checked king can move out of check.
- The checking piece can be captured.
- A friendly piece can block the check.

If one of these methods doesn't get a king out of check, it's checkmate—game over.

Checks can be good or bad moves. In the next position, White has played a bad check. Black can use any of the three methods to get out of check. Of course, capturing White's rook with 1. ... Nxe8 is best.

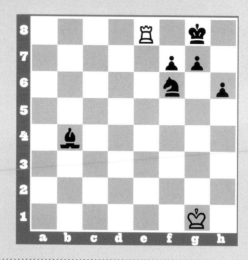

White has given check, but Black has all three ways of getting out of check.

Stalemate

Stalemate is not checkmate! It's a special type of chess position that automatically draws the game. In a stalemate, one side has no legal moves, but the king is *not* in check.

Contrast this position.

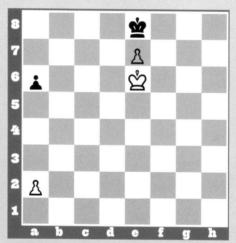

Black to move. Black can move a pawn. So it's not stalemate.

Black to move. Black has no legal moves but is not in check. It's a draw by *stalemate*.

If you have won a lot of extra material, you should win easily by forcing checkmate. But you have to be careful not to fall into a stalemate, which is only a draw.

Black has just played 1. ... Qb3, a very bad move because it stalemates White.

66 **Having collected an army and concentrated his forces, he must blend and harmonize the different elements ...** 99

Chapter 2

First moves

During the opening, a chess general must get the army out of its barracks on the back rank and into battle formation, ready to engage the enemy. In this stage, the two opposing generals feel each other out. Yes, they're alert for a quick kill. But they also know that if the opposing general is experienced, the battle could be long and tough, and every move critical. No movement can be wasted.

Like generals arraying their forces in front of an enemy, chess players can't simply deploy their pawns and pieces at completely preconceived posts. They have to take into consideration the opponent's movements.

Beginnings, middles, and ends

Some chess lovers compare a complete game of chess to a good story. A full game has a beginning that sets the stage, a middle of rising action and complications, and an ending or *denouement* that flows from all that went before to wrap things up logically. Students of the game have found it very helpful to understand that a full chess game does indeed have three stages.

Opening—When the players move a pawn or two and get their pieces to active positions.

Middlegame—Beginning around move 10, after most or all of the pieces have been brought into play.

Endgame—When only a few pieces remain in the battle.

In this chapter, we'll help you play the opening phase of the game like a master strategist.

> ❝ **All armies prefer high ground to low ... It is a military axiom not to advance uphill against the enemy ...** ❞

Armies ancient and modern vied for the high ground of a battlefield. Once an army held it, enemy troops would slow and exhaust themselves climbing to attack. Ever try to throw a spear uphill? We imagine not, but you get the idea.

Taking the high ground

The first stage of chess combat is likewise taking the high ground. On the chessboard the high ground is the four squares in the very center: e4, e5, d4, and d5.

Successful tournament chess players know that the center is prime real estate of the board. "Classical" chess tenets, preached by 19th- and early 20th-century masters, stated flatly that we must occupy the center with pawns early in the game. Later, in the years after World War I, a group of young rebels began to demonstrate that they could win instead by fighting to control the center from a distance. Now we recognize that both approaches are valid. But one way or the other, the center must be a goal.

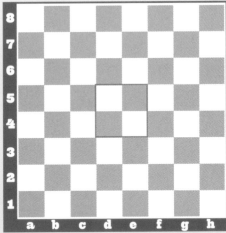

The high ground continues to be important in any military battle. The high ground of the chessboard is the center.

The center is important because it is the crossroads of the ranks and files. If you control the center, you control the movements of both armies. Your pieces can attack in all directions. If you don't have a share of the center, your forces can be divided and left uncoordinated.

Stronger in the center

Occupying the high ground in the center, your pieces exert more influence and have more mobility—a very important military advantage. Compare the number of potential moves a knight has when it's in the center to its mobility when it's "on the rim."

A knight in the center strikes at eight squares all over the board.

A knight in the corner has only two potential moves.

"A knight on the rim is dim," chess players say. Well, "A knight in the corner is even forlorner."

Mistakes made!
Don't ignore your opponent's moves!

Sun Tzu cautions us against preconceived battle plans. Generals and chess players alike have to see and react to the moves of their counterparts across the battlefield or board.

1. e4 e5
So far, so perfect. White stakes out the center. Black also claims a fair share.

2. Qh5 Nc6
White's second move is unorthodox, but not terrible. Black's second move is perfect, guarding the e5 pawn, which the white queen has attacked.

3. Bc4 Nf6??
The double question mark is chess notation indicating that Black's third move is a blunder. Can you see why?

4. Qxf7 checkmate
This sequence occurs so often among beginners that it has a name: Scholar's Mate.

> **66** If you are situated a great distance from the enemy, and the strength of the two armies is equal, it is not easy to provoke a battle, and fighting will be to your disadvantage. **99**

As at the beginning of a military confrontation, or the very start of a chess game—the opening—the distance between armies is at its greatest. The savvy commander builds up his army's pre-combat position move by move, gauging his opponent's actions. Only if one general blunders early, creating a serious weakness, can a sudden attack succeed. Premature attacks launched without such justification will fail and rebound against the attacker.

Three rules for starting the battle

Some important chess ideas, like military concepts, are simple. The difficult part is deciding *when* to apply *which* idea. But in the opening of the game, you can rely on three key stratagems that will guide you to marshal your men like the greatest chessboard general. All three ideas build on your knowledge about the center and are the closest thing to a "winning formula" that we know about in chess.

- Make only one or two pawn moves that occupy and control the center.
- Develop your minor pieces—bishops and knights—to squares that influence the center.
- Castle to get your king into safety for the coming chessboard carnage.

March a center pawn two squares forward to control the center

The two favorite first moves of the chess masters as White are 1. e4 and 1. d4. That's no accident. The two moves have a lot in common.

- Each move *occupies* a center square with a pawn.
- Each move *controls* some enemy territory in the center.
- Each move opens up squares for the queen and a bishop.

Often, a master playing the black pieces will mirror such a move with 1. ... e5 or 1. ... d5 in order to establish a fair share in the high ground of the board.

If you're a newcomer to chess ideas, we recommend that as White, you start your games with 1. e4. As Black, we advocate that you respond to 1. e4 with 1. ... e5 and reply to 1. d4 with 1. ... d5. That way, you get your fair share of the center from the onset of the struggle. These opening moves are time-tested and super-solid.

It's true, as we'll soon see, that there are other opening moves that challenge the center, so, by all means, try out the openings that appeal to you.

Mistakes made!
Heed Sun Tzu's warning to shun premature attacks!

**1. e4 e5 2. Bc4 Nc6
3. Qh5 g6 4. Qf3 Nf6
5. Nc3 Nd4 6. Qd1 Bg7**

White attacked with too few pieces and has been rebuffed. Black is better.

On the first move, push a center pawn out two squares. Here White has played 1. e4, and Black has replied 1. ... e5.

White moved the queen three times only for her to wind up on her original square. Black is well developed and is in control. As Sun Tzu wrote: "The general, unable to control his irritation, will launch his men to the assault like swarming ants, with the result that one-third of his men are slain, while the town still remains untaken."

Here two opposing masters have started the game 1. d4 d5.

Mistakes made! Don't be a rookie!

Beginners frequently want to get their rooks into the game early—perhaps because the rooks are powerful and their moves are easily understood. But doing so is a dreadful idea, like rolling your cannon right into a moat at the start of a battle! A smart chess general waits to see how the siege develops before deciding where the heavy artillery will best be placed.

1. h4? d5 2. Rh3?

White played 1. h4? and 2. Rh3? to get the rook quickly into the game.

In the position above, Black developed in the center with 1. d5 in reaction to White's premature flank attack. White continued with the idea of moving the rook into the battle, ignoring the consequences.

You can see that Black would simply snatch the rook off the board with 2. Bxh3, swapping a three-point minor piece for a five-point major piece. Such an advantageous trade is called "winning the Exchange" (notice the capital "E"). In a game between masters, White would already be considered lost. Not only is White down in material, but kingside castling is now impossible.

Suppose White sees that the rook can't move to h3 and instead continues to try to make the idea work by pushing the h-pawn another square to get away from the reach of the enemy bishop.

3. h5 e5!

White has doubled down on the idea of somehow getting the rook into the game, but Black has reacted wisely with central pawn moves. Notice that Black's queen now covers h4, so there are still no safe squares for White's rook to advance to. This series of moves shows another advantage of moving central pawns forward—*they free up the movement of your bishops and queen.*

Develop minor pieces toward the center

At the beginning of the game, both armies are encamped on their back two rows of the chessboard. Like any good general, you must get your troops into battle array quickly. Otherwise, they can be caught with their backs against the edge of the board, where they have little mobility and no coordination with each other, and can be slaughtered, leading to a quick end for your king.

In the first opening strategy, you sent out a foot soldier to the high ground of the center. And you saw that it's too early to tell where the major pieces can safely be placed. It's time to deploy your minor pieces: the knights and bishops. For a number of reasons, it's easiest to know where a knight will be best developed. In fact it's good to remember the phrase "knight before bishop." Most often White develops the kingside knight first, and the best square is nearly always f3.

Normally, however, modern masters don't bring out *both* knights first, although 100 years ago it was quite common. A modern game that begins with 1. e4 e5 would be more likely to continue

1. e4 e5 2. Nf3 Nc6 3. Bb5 Bc5

Both White and Black have developed a knight and a bishop.

You may at first think that White's third move didn't influence the center, but there's more than one way to do that. Notice that the bishop threatens, at an opportune moment, to capture the knight on c6, removing its defense of the pawn on e5. This opening is called the Ruy Lopez (see page 34).

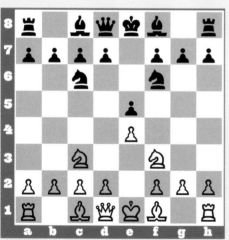

In the opening, the knights are most often best posted on f3, f6, c3, and c6.

Tip The well-developed chess player

Development is a key concept in the chess openings. It means getting your pieces off their home squares and onto more effective ones. Later we'll see that there are two differing approaches to development, *classical* and *hypermodern*. But for now let's stick with classical principles. You must learn these before attempting exceptions. To illustrate them, let's look at what the ideal development for White would be. (The same principles apply to Black.)

The "dream" classical opening development for White.

Castling

Castling does two important things: It whisks your king into safety and brings your rook toward the center, where it can exert meaningful influence. As a general rule, it's best to castle within the first 10 moves of the game. We acknowledge that there may be pressing concerns as the enemy's pieces are deployed against yours in the early skirmishing. But once you've cleared the back rank between your king and a rook, look for the opportunity to castle. In most games, masters castle kingside.

In fact, in the position given in the right-hand column of page 29, White's best move is to castle:

4. 0-0

White has castled kingside.

If both sides followed "book"—that's how veteran chess players describe making opening moves that are frequently played by the leading grandmasters—these could be the next few moves:

4. ... Nf6 5. Nc3 0-0

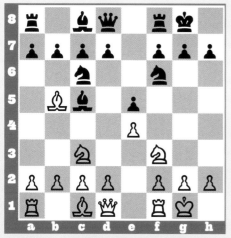

Masterful opening play. Both sides have staked out the center with a pawn, developed minor pieces, and castled.

Chapter 3

Openings and their centers

66 The natural formation of the country is the soldier's best ally. 99

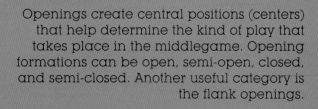

Openings create central positions (centers) that help determine the kind of play that takes place in the middlegame. Opening formations can be open, semi-open, closed, and semi-closed. Another useful category is the flank openings.

This chapter looks at the specific initial chess moves that make up the openings. Experienced chess players have their favorite beginnings. It's true that highly rated players even have many lines of move-and-response (called variations) in a specific opening memorized. But learning an opening is much more about studying the themes— the strategic and tactical ideas—that occur and recur in an opening. What's more, it's very important to know the kinds of positions that evolve from an opening. In fact, chess players cherish their favorite openings largely because they feel comfortable in the resulting middlegames—the complicated battles that come after the opening.

Before we go any further, we want to make two ideas very clear. First, because it takes decisions from both players to create an opening, many openings can start out looking like one opening and wind up being another. When that happens, we say the game has "transposed" into a certain opening. Second, we must caution you not to become too fascinated with opening study. There are hundreds of books written on specific opening variations, but the basics we cover here will take you far. Even if you become a serious tournament player, don't spend more than 25 percent of your time on openings. It's true that you want to get off to a good start. But there are lots of other valuable ideas still to learn.

> **❝ Ground on which each side has liberty of movement is open ground. ❞**

Like any good military general, a chess player must react to the formations mustered by the enemy.

Open games

Chess battles that begin with 1. e4 e5 are called open games because they generally result in positions that have open files and diagonals for pieces to exert long-range influence.

The Ruy Lopez is an open game popular with masters. Named after a 16-century Spanish priest who analyzed it, it's also known as the Spanish Opening—and sometimes, only half-jokingly, as The Spanish Torture.

1. e4 e5 2. Nf3 Nc6 3. Bb5

The Ruy Lopez opening

White's third move is an indirect threat, undermining the knight that protects Black's center pawn. But if you want to try it out, one of the first things you should understand is that White can't win the e5-pawn right away.

For example, after

3. ... a6 4. Bxc6 dxc6 5. Nxe5? Qd4!

Black will win back the pawn with a good game. Notice that even after the alternative 4. ... bxc6 5. Nxe5?, Black has 5. ... Qe7, winning back the pawn with a good position. After 3. ... Nf6, another popular response to the Ruy Lopez, Black would answer a too-soon try to win the center pawn in the same way.

Both White and Black have a number of very sound ways of continuing in the Ruy. You'll see some of them later in the book as we cover other chess ideas.

The Italian Game is another complex of open games that begins when White chooses on the third move to place the bishop on c4 instead of b5. There is no indirectness here; White's intentions are aggressive, aiming at Black's sensitive f7 square, the black king's weak spot before the black army is mobilized. Black has two popular ways to respond. He can play 3. ... Nf6, entering the aggressive and complicated Two Knights Defense. Or he can reply with 3. ... Bc5, giving us the Giuoco Piano, the oldest recorded opening. Its name is Italian for "Quiet Game," which is ironic because it can be anything but quiet.

By the way, you've just read why it takes two to make an opening. Both sides have choices. Neither White nor Black can force any one opening on the other.

1. e4 e5 2. Nf3 Nc6 3. Bc4 Bc5

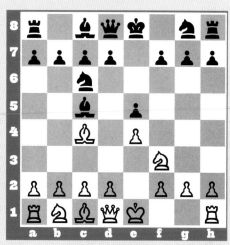

The Giuoco Piano opening

In this seemingly simple position, White has a half-dozen choices on the next move. He often plays 4. c3, threatening to build a big center with 5. d4, often sacrificing a pawn for the initiative. Yet another popular gambit is 4. d4 right away. Even more speculative is 4. b4, the Evans Gambit, popular long ago and still dangerous, in which White offers a gambit pawn to speed up development. Still another option is 4. 0-0, offering the e4-pawn for a lead in development. Much more conservative is the move 4. e3, the Giuoco Pianissimo (Very Quiet Game), which signals White's intent to build up slowly.

Other notable open game beginnings:

**The Two Knights' Defense: 1. e4 e5
2. Nf3 Nc6 3. Bc4 Nf6**

White usually continues 4. Ng5 or 4.
d4. Black must know a lot of theory!

Petrov's Defense: 1. e4 e5 2. Nf3 Nf6

Black chooses an immediate
counter-attack. After 3. Nxe5, Black
should play 3. ... d6, and only
after 4. Nf3, capture the pawn with
4. ... Nxe4.

The Philidor Defense: 1. e4 e5 2. Nf3 d6

Black defends e5 by moving the
pawn to d6 rather than developing
his knight to c6. White normally
continues with 3. d4.

The Bishop's Opening: 1. e4 e5 2. Bc4

White violates the "knight before
bishop" rule to restrain ... d5 and
leave open the possibility of an early
f4. With 2. ... Nf6, Black narrows
White's choices.

The Scotch Game: 1. e4 e5 2. Nf3 Nc6 3. d4

After 3. … exd4, White can recapture immediately with 4. Nxd4 or play the Scotch Gambit with 4. Bc4.

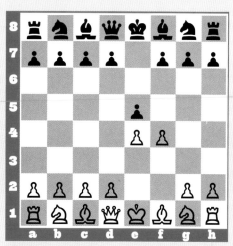

The King's Gambit: 1. e4 e5 2. f4

Risky play from a romantic era—Black can accept the gambit or decline it. An interesting counter-gambit is 2. … d5 3. exd5 c6!?. If 4. fxe4? Qh4+!.

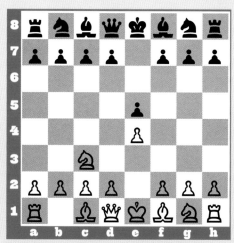

The Vienna Game: 1. e4 e5 2. Nc3

White doesn't take the initiative by attacking e5. Instead, the plan is f4 or g3 with Bg2. Black can continue with 2. … Nf6 or 2. … Nc6.

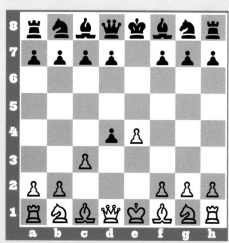

The Danish Gambit: 1. e4 e5 2. d4 exd4 3. c3

Black can accept the pawn sacrifice with 3. … dxc3 or safely decline it with the counter-thrust 3. … d5.

> **❝ ... a power of estimating the adversary, of controlling the forces of victory, and of shrewdly calculating difficulties, dangers and distances constitutes the test of a great general. ❞**

The quote from Sun Tzu is a hallmark of successful play in the challenging semi-open positions. These debuts are a real test of the generalship of both players. All openings have pluses and minuses. One way to understand the semi-open games is to realize that both the positives and negatives are magnified.

Semi-open games

When White plays 1. e4 and Black responds with any move but 1. ... e5, it's a semi-open game. Semi-open games are the hallmark of dynamic modern chess. Black doesn't try to negate each of White's moves, but sets out on move 1 to accumulate a separate set of advantages. The Sicilian Defense is the most popular reply to 1. e4 among today's top players, ahead of 1. ... e5.

The Sicilian Defense

Black plays for an immediate imbalance while controlling e5. Although Black doesn't immediately open up diagonals for the pieces, the move has a different plus: If White advances the d-pawn to d4, which usually follows, Black will trade a wing pawn for a center pawn, theoretically an advantageous swap. Because of the Sicilian's subtlety and popularity, master play has developed many fascinating variations of the opening. For now, let's look at a few moves of one of the most time-tested and popular, the Najdorf Sicilian, named after the Polish-Argentinian grandmaster Miguel Najdorf.

1. e4 c5 2. Nf3 d6 3. d4 cxd4 4. Nxd4 Nf6 5. Nc3 a6

It's true that Black's play seems to flout the classical principles you've studied. Black is moving wing pawns and has developed only one piece. But this is a delicate game of cat-and-mouse with White, denying White's access to b5, normally attractive to a knight or bishop. Black relies on the structural advantage of an extra center pawn, and will often advance on the queenside with b5 and *fianchetto* the bishop on b7. (*Fianchetto*, from

the Italian for "little flank," means to deploy a bishop in a hypermodern way—as White on either g2 or b2, as Black on g7 or b7.)

6. Bg5 e6 7. f4 Qb6 8. Qd2

The Poisoned Pawn Variation

We couldn't show you the Sicilian without a look at one of the most contested positions in modern chess: the Poisoned Pawn Variation. (A white *en prise* pawn on b2 has the reputation of often being toxic—dangerous to capture.) After **8. ... Qxb2**, and either 9. Rb1 or 9. Nc3, Black has an extra pawn, but White has dangerous chances to take advantage of Black's most powerful piece being off-sides. Even Bobby Fischer, one of the foremost advocates of this ultra-sharp defense, lost a rare game after taking the pawn in his otherwise successful 1972 World Championship match against the Russian Boris Spassky.

The French Defense: 1. e4 e6 2. d4 d5

In the French Defense, Black supports the center but blocks in his light-squared bishop. Black's game can be initially cramped, but it is possible to use the c- and f-pawns to undermine White's center. In many games, Black's play lies on the queenside while White attacks on the kingside.

The Caro–Kann Defense: 1. e4 c6 2. d4 d5

In the Caro–Kann Defense, Black gives the light-squared bishop an open diagonal, but doesn't forward kingside development. It's a solid defense chosen by players who look forward to the endgame and, to get there, are willing to endure White's freer play in the opening and middlegame.

The Pirc Defense

The Pirc Defense arises after **1. e4 d6 2. d4 Nf6 3. Nc3 g6**. Its idea is to allow White to commit to the "ideal" center, and then attack it. The group of openings that share this approach is known as hypermodern openings. They are sound and challenging for both sides, but they give White a very wide choice in the deployment of forces, requiring Black to be prepared and confident in many kinds of variations.

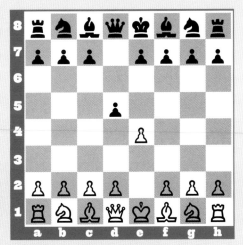

The Scandinavian Defense: 1. e4 d5

In the Scandinavian Defense, after **2. exd5 Qxd5**, Black's queen is exposed to attack as White develops the minor pieces, most often with **3. Nc3**. But Black enjoys good piece play and the defense is sound—and can be especially effective as a surprise.

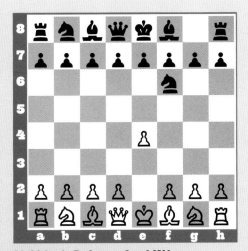

Alekhine's Defense: 1. e4 Nf6

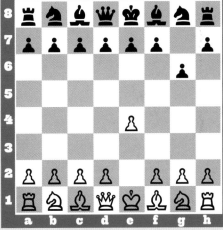

The Modern Defense: 1. e4 g6

Alekhine's Defense is another hypermodern concept. After **1. e4 Nf6**, White can chase the knight with pawns and even build a massive pawn center after 2. e5 Nd5 3. d4 d6 4. c4 Nb6 5. f4. Few modern masters as White will now choose this extreme "punishment," however, preferring to build a smaller, less vulnerable, but still classical, center. Players of the black pieces, like their cousins who play the Pirc or other hypermodern openings, thrive on the challenge of undermining classical centers.

The Modern Defense (that's just a name that stuck; the defense is now an old idea) is the ultimate stick-in-the-eye to classical chess ideology. After **1.e4 g6**, White's burden is the plethora of choices. Once again, Black is looking to counter-punch against a broad pawn center. In doing so, Black is walking a tightrope over the Grand Canyon without a safety net. It is possible to make it to the other side, but any slight misstep can be fatal.

66 With regard to narrow passes, if you can occupy them first, let them be strongly garrisoned and await the advent of the enemy. 99

The Battle at Thermopylae, Greek for "The Hot Gates," in 480 BCE is the most famous example of fighting in narrow straits. For three days, a mere 7,000 Greeks led by the Spartan commander Leonidas held off a Persian army of some 150,000 under the Persian king Xerxes. In closed games, a chess player must be wary of a costly frontal assault like Xerxes', since the chess armies start out equal.

Closed games

Closed openings begin with 1. d4 d5. Although this may at first remind you of the Open Games, the resulting character of the play is normally very different. White's first move can be said to be more conservative, as it occupies the center with a pawn that is protected by the queen (the e-pawn has no such protection after 1. e4). The *grande dame* of the closed games is the Queen's Gambit, a mainstay of masters for hundreds of years.

1. d4 d5 2. c4

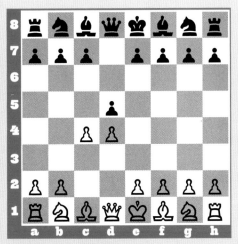

The Queen's Gambit

White threatens to trade a wing pawn for Black's center pawn. Together with the first move, that could turn out to be a serious opening advantage.

Black has many ways of continuing. The offered pawn can be captured—that's called the *Queen's Gambit Accepted*. Or Black can defend the center with 1. ... e6 or 1. ... d6, to cite just a couple of alternatives. But most modern masters tired of defending the more-or-less thankless positions that ensue, in which frequently the best result they could hope for was a

draw. We'll see some of the dynamic alternatives they developed in the section on semi-closed games.

Also included in the closed games are openings that begin 1. d4 d5 in which White makes another choice, such as 2. Nf3, 2. e3, or 2. Bf4.

Tip When is a gambit not a gambit?

Sometimes opening nomenclature is arbitrary. The Modern Defense is hundreds of years old, the Orang Utan (1. b4) was named after a visit to the zoo, and the Queen's Gambit is not actually a gambit! Black can't capture the pawn on c4 and successfully keep it. It's instructive to see why.

2. ... dxc4 3. e3 b5 4. a4 c6! 5. axb5 cxb5? 6. Qf3

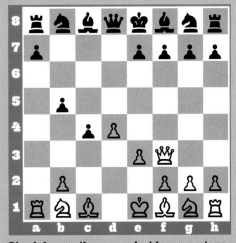

Black keeps the pawn but loses a piece.

White's last move attacks the *en prise* rook. The best Black can do is lose a knight after 6. ... Nc6 7. Qxc6+ Bd7.

> **66 Ground which can be abandoned but is hard to re-occupy is called ENTANGLING. ... if the enemy is prepared for your coming, and you fail to defeat him, then, return being impossible, disaster will ensue. 99**

In Sun Tzu's terms, the center and adjacent squares are the "entangling ground." Once ceded, they are often difficult to occupy. This group of openings includes any response to 1. d4 that is not the symmetrical 1. d5. Black abandons the center at least temporarily—and that's the key.

Semi-closed games

Modern masters looked for dynamic alternatives to classical symmetry against 1. e4. They did the same against 1. ... d4. The most important group is called Indian Openings, because many feature a bishop fianchetto by Black, a maneuver that was popularized in the 19th century by players from India. All Indian defenses start with **1. d4 Nf6.**

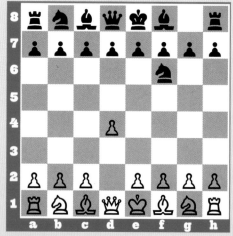

The Indians are coming.

Black develops a piece and prevents White from immediately dominating the center with 2. e4. From here, the game can take many forms.

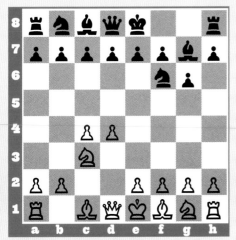

The King's Indian Defense

The Nimzo-Indian Defense

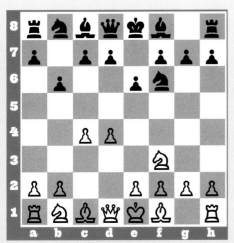

The Queen's Indian Defense

The Benoni Defense

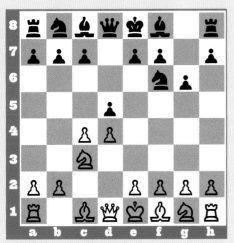

The Grünfeld Defense

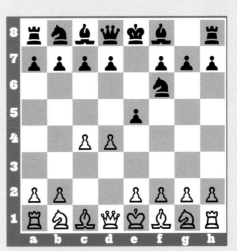

The Budapest Counter-Gambit

> **❝ The direct and the indirect lead on to each other in turn. It is like moving in a circle—you never come to an end. Who can exhaust the possibilities of their combination? ❞**

Sun Tzu teaches us that it's not only the most direct move that can obtain an objective. Flank openings are a chessboard example. You've already learned that controlling the center, rather than occupying it, is another way to fight for the high ground. The flank openings take this approach.

Flank openings

When White, on the first move, advances a non-center pawn, we call it a flank opening. As always in non-classical openings, the other side is given wide latitude in its choices, leaving plenty of accessible ground for either army. In part, that's the challenge to Black: Take up the gauntlet and occupy the center immediately, knowing that White is waiting to counter-punch? Or, should Black play it cagey and wait for White's intentions to be declared?

Flank openings appeal to creative players who want to go their own way or who want to catch their opponents unprepared. A good reaction is to stick with classical principles: Advance a center pawn, develop, and castle: one, two, three.

The English Opening: 1. c4

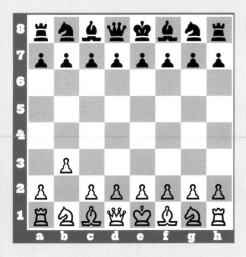

Larsen's Opening:
1. b3

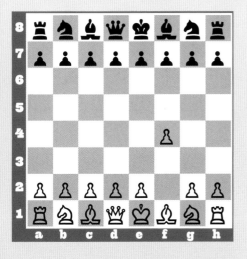

Bird's Opening:
1. f4

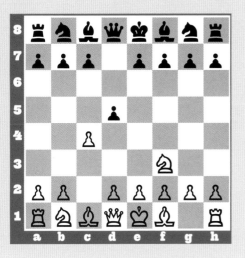

The Réti Opening:
1. Nf3 d5 2. c4

Tip In any play, you must know your lines

As a chess player, you'll want an opening repertoire—a set of openings that you like the feel of and that you have experience with. You want to go into a game with ideas about what you want to play as White—we recommend you start with 1. e4 ("Best by test!"—Bobby Fischer) so that you will gain experience with tactics in the open games.

As Black, you should have a defense to 1. e4 and 1. d4, the most common openings you'll face when you sit across from a worthy opponent.

Like any military commander, you can deal confidently with strange moves and unorthodox strategies by applying what you've learned from the ideas in this book and from experience.

> **66** Hence the skillful fighter puts himself into a position which makes defeat impossible, and does not miss the moment for defeating the enemy. **99**

Chess games can be long or short. Sometimes, as in military encounters, the fight can be over in a flash of attack when one side makes a blunder in the initial deployment of his troops. Be mindful of good development in the opening to protect yourself from early defeats. And be ever alert for such a mistake by your opponent.

Practice puzzles

How quickly can blunders in the opening lead to a rout? Find the winning ideas in the positions below and you'll see. Solutions are given on pages 50–51. Refer to pages 54–61 for guidance on tactics used.

①

Black to move

②

Black to move

3

White to move

5

Black to move

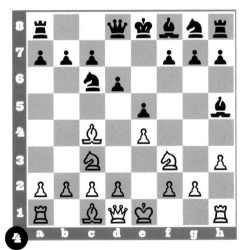

4

White to move

6

Black to move

Solutions to puzzles on previous pages

1. Deadly sidelong glance

4. ... Qa5+!. Black's queen springs from her throne to launch a double attack, giving check on the diagonal while targeting the knight on the rank. White must block the check. On his next move, Black will capture the knight on e5.

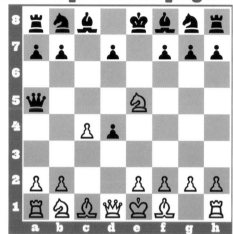

Position after 4. ... Qa5+!

The game began: 1. d4 c5 2. c4 cxd4 3. Nf3 e5 4. Nxe5? (4. e3 is White's best, offering a gambit pawn in exchange for development).

2. Noah's Ark trap

4. ... b5! 5. Bb3 c4!. White's bishop is trapped behind the black phalanx of pawns.

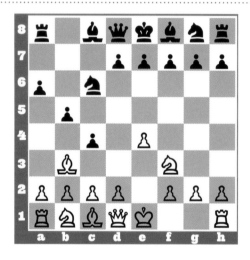

This one started: 1. e4 c5 2. Nf3 Nc6 3. Bb5 a6 4. Ba4 (4. Bxc6 was White's best move to avoid losing the bishop). This ancient bishop-waylaying ambush can be sprung in a number of openings. It's especially prevalent in the Ruy Lopez. The name may come from the idea that the trap is as old as Noah's Ark.

3. Fork and knife

This one's a bit of a variation on the first puzzle, combining two tactics—first a fork (see page 55), which doesn't seem effective, followed by the queen stabbing at Black's position with a double attack.

5. e4! Bxe4 6. Qa4+. White wins the bishop on e4.

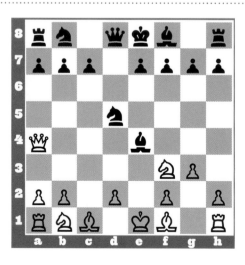

The position arose after: 1. Nf3 d5 2. g3 Bf5 3. c4 Nf6 4. cxd5 Nxd5? (4. ... Qxd5 or even 4. ... c6, continuing in gambit fashion, is better).

4. It shouldn't be legal

6. Nxe5! Bxd1? 7. Bxf7+ Ke7 8. Nd5#. This stunning early checkmate is called Legall's Mate and has claimed many victims for hundreds of years. The pattern is named after the great French player Legall de Kermeur (1702–92).

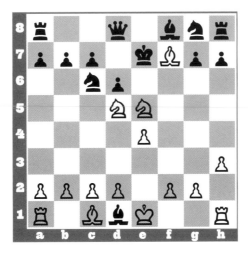

The trap can develop in a number of ways. This variation began: 1. e4 e5 2. Nf3 Nc6 3. Bc4 d6 4. Nc3 Bg4 5. h3 Bh5? (Black is much better off capturing on f3 rather than retreating the bishop). After 6. Nxe5!, it's hard for Black to resist 6. ... Bxd1?, but 6. ... Nxe5 is better, although still losing: 7. Qxh5 g6 (if 7. ... Nxc4 8. Qb5+) 8. Qe2, when White is a healthy pawn ahead.

5. Elephant trap

6. ... Nxd5! 7. Bxd8 Bb4+ 8. Qd2 Bxd2+ 9. Kxd2 Kxd8. Black comes out of the exchanges a piece ahead.

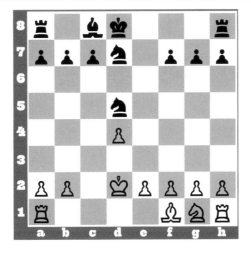

This is another old trap, with a name that suggests catching big game. It comes out of the Queen's Gambit Declined: 1. d4 d5 2. c4 e6 3. Nc3 Nf6 4. Bg5 Nbd7 5. cxd5 exd5 6. Nxd5?. (White thinks the pin on f6 allows a valuable center pawn to be captured. But 6. e3 or 6. Nf3 is best, with a sound game for White.)

6. Lack of development

4. ... Bxf2+ 5. Kxf2 Ne4+ 6. Kf3 (6. Ke3 is better but still loses after 6. ... Qh4 7. g4 Nf2) **6. ... Qh4 7. g3** (if 7. g4 f5!) **7. ... Qxg3+ 8. Kxe4 f5+! 9. Kxf5 d6+ 10. Ke4 Bf5+! 11. Kxf5 Qg6#.** This was all played in a correspondence game, a game played by mail, in 1952.

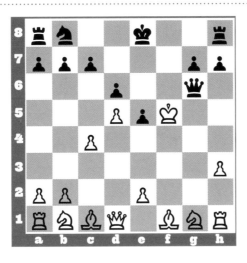

The opening is a Budapest Defense: 1. d4 Nf6 2. c4 e5 3. d5 (3. dxe5 is much better, making Black spend time to try to recover his gambit pawn) 3. ... Bc5 4. h3. White has totally ignored development and weakened the dark squares on two diagonals, allowing the pretty bishop sacrifice.

❝ The skillful tactician may be likened to the SHUAI-JAN snake that is found in the Ch'ang mountains. Strike at its head, and you will be attacked by its tail; strike at its tail, and you will be attacked by its head; strike at its middle, and you will be attacked by head and tail both. ❞

Chapter 4
Tactics

Tactics are indeed the snakebites of chess—the quick strikes that win material or gain you some other advantage. Tactics are short-term actions, as opposed to strategy, which is long-term planning. Of course, all military campaigns are made up of both tactics and strategy.

A famous old chess master once wrote "Chess is 99 percent tactics." That's truth through hyperbole, making the point that the most profound overall war strategy is meaningless unless you win the skirmishes on a hand-to-hand level.

Most tactics are used to win material. In chess, the overall goal is always checkmate, but having more material than your opponent makes forcing checkmate a lot easier—and often inevitable!

In this chapter, we'll look at tactics, the working tools of winning chess.

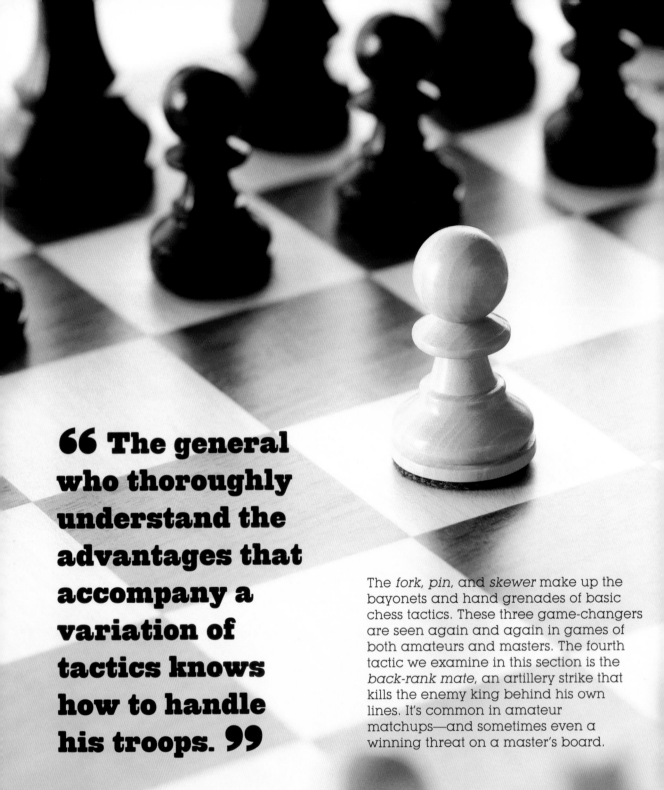

66 The general who thoroughly understand the advantages that accompany a variation of tactics knows how to handle his troops. 99

The *fork*, *pin*, and *skewer* make up the bayonets and hand grenades of basic chess tactics. These three game-changers are seen again and again in games of both amateurs and masters. The fourth tactic we examine in this section is the *back-rank mate*, an artillery strike that kills the enemy king behind his own lines. It's common in amateur matchups—and sometimes even a winning threat on a master's board.

The popular four

Let's start out with four of the most common, workhorse tactics that appear in a great many chess games.

Double attack (fork)

A double attack, or fork, is a single move that makes two threats at the same time. In medieval times, most forks had only two tines. Envision that, or think of a fork in the road. Then look at this position:

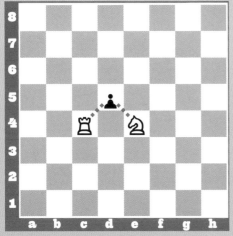

A double attack in its simplest form.

You can see that the pawn attacks two pieces at once. No matter which white piece moves, the black pawn will capture the other one.

Any chess piece can give a double attack. Perhaps the most dreaded double attack is executed by knights, because of their tricky way of moving. Although the terms *double attack* and *fork* mean the same thing, the knight's double attack is nearly always called a fork. In the diagram below, White has forked Black's king and queen. The king must move, and White will play 1. Nxc8.

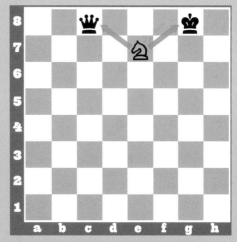

White has executed the royal fork, attacking the king and queen simultaneously.

Mistakes made!
Don't leave them hanging!

Beginners have to learn to check carefully to make sure they do not move or leave pieces on squares where they are attacked and not defended. "Look twice, move once," should be your watchword. We use the French phrase *en prise* (pronounced "ahn preez") to indicate a piece that can be taken for free. We also say such pieces are "hanging." Permitting such a capture is a blunder, of course, that should cost you the game.

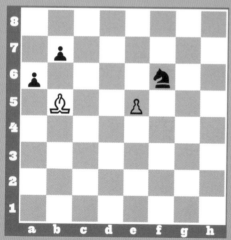

White's bishop is hanging. Black's knight is also *en prise*.

Pin

A pin attacks an enemy piece, but the threatened piece can't move because that would expose a more valuable piece. Hence the name "pin."

White's bishop pins the black knight.

Back-rank mate

This is instant death to the king. A queen or a rook attacks an unprotected king on its own back rank, where it is hemmed in by his own pawns. This can suddenly happen in the middle of a game with many pieces on the board. Watch for it!

Skewer

The skewer is the flipside of the pin. Think of it as a chess-piece shish kabob. The more valuable piece is attacked and forced to move, exposing a less valuable piece behind it.

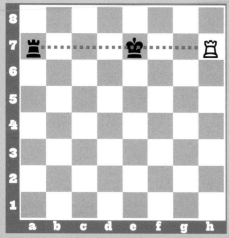

A skewer: White's rook attacks the black king, which must move, exposing the undefended black rook to capture.

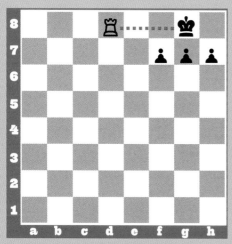

Back-rank mate. Black has lost.

Tip Counting attackers and defenders

Counting how many times a chessman is attacked by enemy pieces *of the same value*—and comparing that number to how many times it is defended—is a basic tactical skill. To win material successfully in such cases, a player must have one more attacker than defender. In this diagram, Black is in danger of losing the pawn to 1. Rxc5. But it's Black's move.

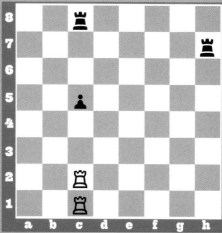

Black's pawn is attacked twice but defended only once. It can be defended again with 1. ... Rhc7.

> ❝ **Reduce the hostile chiefs by inflicting damage on them; make trouble for them, and keep them constantly engaged; hold out specious allurements, and make them rush to any given point.** ❞

"Specious allurements" is the perfect phrase for the next two chess tactics. Decoys have always been a part of warfare. In World War II, the so-called Ghost Army literally used rubber blowups and artwork to make the Germans think the Allied armies were in one spot when they were actually someplace else. Deflection is another chessboard tactic that misdirects enemy forces—into a waiting minefield.

Lures and snares

In this section, we'll look at two crafty tactics that are a bit higher on the ladder of sophistication. Both have to do with forcing your enemy to put an important piece on the wrong square—for your opponent! Sun Tzu would be proud.

Decoy

When you get your opponent to move a piece *to the square you want it on*, that's a *decoy*. In the position below, White sacrifices the rook for a lowly pawn in order to decoy the enemy queen to a square that will set up a knockout blow.

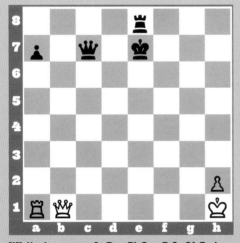

White to move: **1. Rxa7! Qxa7 2. Qh7+!**

Set up the above position on your own board and study it. Notice that if White instead played 1. Qh7+, Black could play 1. ... Kd8, guarding the queen and making things a bit more complicated. White first needed to decoy the black queen to a more distant square on the seventh rank, just out of reach of such a defense.

Deflection

When you get your opponent to move a piece *away from* an important square, that's *deflection*. The position below brings together a number of concepts you've learned.

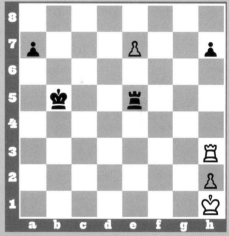

1. Rh5! RxRh5 2. e8=Q+

A fork! Wherever Black moves the king, White plays **3. Qxh4**, a queen ahead. Go over this position on your own board and you'll review some key chess ideas: the initial deflection is followed by promotion with a double attack that puts Black in check.

66 All warfare is based on deception. 99

Our last bandolier of chess ammunition contains three tactics that seem to the enemy to come out of nowhere. All of our discussions of tactics give you ideas for winning material. But they should also help you stay out of your opponents' snares.

Overloading

It's a mistake to give too many duties to one soldier. The same goes for a chessman. Overloading is actually a theme that invites tactics. When a piece is overloaded with important obligations, it's a target for a trick.

To solve the position below, you'll need to make use of several things you've learned in this chapter. Notice that Black's bishop guards two *back-rank mating* squares, one each from White's rooks, on e8 and a8.

Did you find the *deflection* **1. Ra8+**, which requires Black to play **1. ... Bxa8** to avoid immediate mate? Unfortunately for Black, White then has **2. Re8 checkmate**, because Black's overloaded defender has been deflected.

Black had no options. The above line of play is an example of a *combination*. A combination is a series of forced moves to gain an advantage—in this case, checkmate.

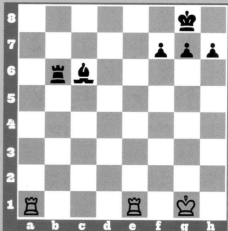

White to move. Find the tactic on the overloaded black bishop.

Double check

Double check is the nuclear missile of the chessboard. It's a special form of discovered attack. One piece moves, giving check. And at the same time, another piece is uncovered that also gives check.

Here's an actual game from 1855. White is Alexander Meek, an American politician, lawyer, judge, poet—and chess player. Notice that in the initial position, Meek's queen is *en prise* to the black bishop on f3.

In-between move

This tactic may be the ultimate chessboard surprise. Your opponent makes a move and thinks your reply is forced and automatic. But you deliver a shock by making a different move before making the supposedly forced move. I'm sure you've noticed that our examples are getting more complicated.

Here's an example from a game between the current World Champion, Magnus Carlsen, of Norway (white), and the US Champion Hikaru Nakamura. Black has just played **37. ... Rxc1.**

White to move: 1. Nf6+!, double check and mate!

After 1. Nf6+ White's queen, which is now giving check as a result of a discovered attack, actually remains *en prise*. But Black doesn't have time to capture it because Black's king is also in check from the knight. That's the power of double check! Note that the only way to escape from a double check is to move the king— you can't take two pieces or block both checks with one move.

The American champion could have expected an automatic 38. Qxc1, after which 38. ... Qxd6 results in approximate equality. Instead White uncorked the in-between move **39. Rxg6!+**, winning a pawn. Since it's check, Black is compelled to deal with the threat immediately. After 39. ... hxg6, only then did White have to play 40. Qxc1. In the interim, he had netted a valuable pawn and went on to win.

Master games

Both of the following games are masterpieces painted with tactics. In both, Black allowed his forces to lose touch with each other—to fail to coordinate as an army. A chess master, like a commander in the field, must make sure every element under his command serves one purpose.

> **❝ In war, then, let your great object be victory, not lengthy campaigns. ❞**

Chess players put the following game in the category of "miniatures," usually games of under 20 moves. This one is a mere 11! Richard Reti expends his queen, his most powerful piece, on move 9 to force checkmate. He knows, as Sun Tzu reminds us, that victory is not about the length of the campaign.

Blindsided

This game between two great masters of the olden days of classical chess is still replayed by thousands of chess lovers. Many know it by heart.

RICHARD RÉTI (CZECHOSLOVAKIA) V
SAVIELLY TARTAKOWER (POLAND)
VIENNA, 1910

1. e4 c6 2. d4 d5
You'll recall from Chapter 3 that this opening is called the Caro-Kann. It's a sensible debut, bracing Black's stake in the center with c6.

3. Nc3 dxe4 4. Nxe4 Nf6
5. Qd3 e5?

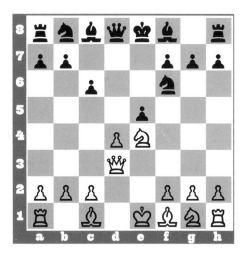

Black inadvisably opens up the game when his opponent is better developed. Instead, 5. ... Nbd7 or 5. ... Nxe4 would have been safer.

continued on next page

6. dxe5 Qa5+ 7. Bd2 Qxe5
8. 0-0-0 Nxe4?

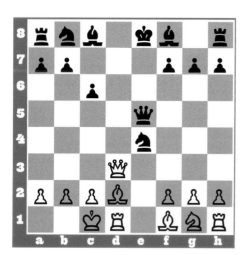

Asking for trouble in the open center!
Developing and protecting his king
with **8. ... Be7** would have been
much better. White would have an
advantage in development, but
there would have been a fight.

9. Qd8+!

Tactics are a product of a better
position. White is much better
developed and Black has neglected
the safety of his king. Here the
winning tactic is a decoy—in the
form of a beautiful queen sacrifice
that can't be declined!

9. ... Kxd8 10. Bg5+

A discovered attack that gives
double check!

10. ... Kc7

If 10. ... Ke8, then 11. Rd8#.

11. Bd8#

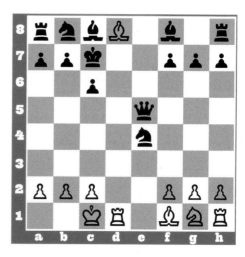

Checkmate! The lesson—don't open
up the game when your opponent is
better developed!

66 If his forces are united, separate them. 99

Paul Morphy taught us how to put the enemy forces into disarray with one tactical threat after another, as he does throughout the following game. One standout example is the position after Black's move 14. Just when it seems Black will pull his troops together, Morphy puts them into ineffective chaos.

A night at the opera

This game is even more famous than the last. It was played by Paul Morphy, who some consider the greatest chess talent of all time. See if you can keep track of his use of the various tactics you've just studied.

A bit of interesting background: Morphy, just a young man of 21, was celebrated as the unofficial World Champion. Two admirers in Paris took him to the opera. Legend has it that they seated their young opponent with his back to the stage and insisted on a chess game in which the two strong amateur players could consult against him. So Morphy was in a hurry to finish and watch the show.

PAUL MORPHY (USA) v **DUKE OF BRUNSWICK** (GERMANY) AND **COUNT ISOUARD** (FRANCE)
PARIS, 1858

1. e4 e5 2. Nf3 d6
You will recognize the Philidor Defense from page 36. Black bolsters the central pawn on e5 while opening a diagonal for the light-squared bishop.

3. d4
We've seen that the initiative is very important in the opening. Morphy keeps the initiative by attacking e5 again. Black must react, so there is no time for Black to make threats. If Black plays 3. ... exd4, White's knight recaptures with 4. Nxd4, taking up a central post.

3. ... Bg4
Black pins the knight to keep White from winning the e5–pawn.

continued on next page

4. dxe5 Bxf3 5. Qxf3 dxe5
6. Bc4

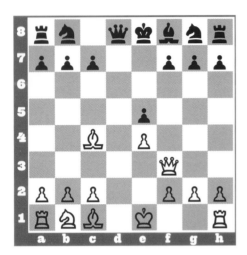

Threatening 7. Qxf7 checkmate.

6. ... Nf6 7. Qb3!

Notice the double attack on f7 and b7.

7. ... Qe7 8. Nc3 c6 9. Bg5

White pins the knight to the queen, immobilizing the horseman.

9. ... b5

Black is eager to push White's bishop off c4.

10. Nxb5!

Morphy sacrifices his knight to keep Black's king a hunted man on the central files.

10. ... cxb5 11. Bxb5+ Nbd7
12. 0–0–0 Rd8

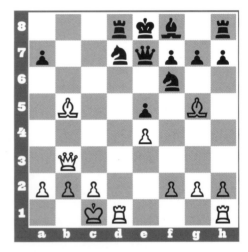

13. Rxd7 Rxd7

White has sacrificed the Exchange (rook for minor piece) to maintain the deadly pin on d7.

14. Rd1

Morphy rushes his last reserve unit into the battle. Even though White is down in material, he has four pieces in the action, while half of Black's army is still encamped!

14. ... Qe6 15. Bxd7+ Nxd7

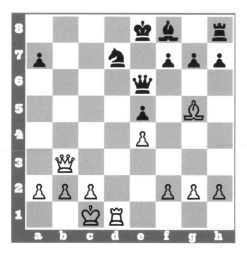

Poor Black. Morphy's opponents have an extra piece and can finally plan to move their bishop with the thought of castling his majesty into safety. But Morphy delivers a crushing game-ender.

16. Qb8+

A queen sacrifice to deflect a key defender!

16. ... Nxb8 17. Rd8#

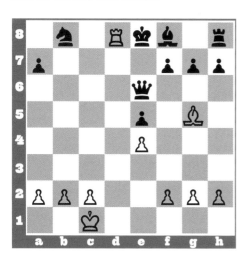

Morphy's use of tactics left his opponents reeling from one hurried defensive try to another. Black was never able to castle. In the end, Black remained with a huge collection of useless material, as White's remaining two pieces performed an elegant checkmate!

" He who knows these things, and in fighting puts his knowledge into practice, will win his battles. He who knows them not, nor practises them, will surely be defeated. "

Military leaders of all eras fought practice battles. So do chess masters. In fact, they never stop solving tactical puzzles to keep themselves sharp and battle-ready.

Practice puzzles

In each of the positions below, there is a winning tactical idea. Study the positions carefully. It helps to set them up on your own board. You'll see that even great champions can lose to "simple" tactics.

   Whether or not you think you've solved each puzzle, go over its solution on pages 70–71 to make sure you thoroughly understand how a tactic won the game.

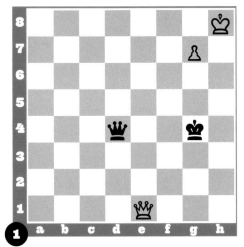

1 White to move

2 White to move

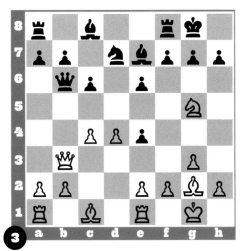

3 Black to move

4 White to move

Solutions to puzzles on previous page

1. Few pieces but lots of tactics
In the puzzle's position, only a few pieces remain on the board, and yet we'll see a pin, a double attack, a pawn promotion, and a skewer!

White would love to advance the pawn, promoting it to a queen with **1. g8Q+**, but can't do so because the pawn is pinned to the king by the black queen. So White finds a double attack that decoys the black queen: **1. Qg1+!**. Black's next move is forced, since it's capture or be captured: **1. ... Qxg1**. So now what? White has sacrificed the queen—there'd better be something to show for it. **2. g8=Q+!**. A skewer! Black must move the king, then White will capture Black's queen and wind up a queen ahead—an easy win.

2. A sharp eye nabs the queen
The puzzle shows an opening position from an actual game between rated experts. Let's go back one move for each side to see how this position occured.

White to move

Here White played 1. e5!. Now if Black could resist being greedy and play 1. ... Ng4, the game would remain roughly equal. But Black snatched the pawn with **1. ... dxe5?**. That gives us the puzzle's position and allows **2. Bxf7!+**. The black king has only one move, **2. ... Kxf7**. Do you see the deflection? Without the king guarding her, the black queen is *en prise*: **3. Qxd8** acquires an overwhelming material advantage.

3. Double trouble

The third puzzle position is a game from one of the top boards at the 1989 US Open Championship. International Grandmaster Dmitry Gurevich as White faced the new defector from the old Soviet Union, 15-year-old Gata Kamsky, later to become a US Champion and World Championship contender. Did you see how the teenager wins a piece? **1. ... Qa5!** executes a double attack on the white rook on e1 and the white knight on g5. (Did you count to see that the knight is now attacked twice and defended only once?) If White tries 2. Qc3, Black replies 2. ... Bb4.

4. World championship in-between moves

The final puzzle position is actually from a game by then-current World Champion Max Euwe of the Netherlands. Let's go back to see how the position occurred.

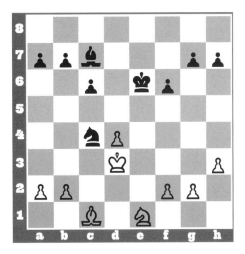

White, former World Champion Emanuel Lasker, has just played 1. Kd3, attacking Black's knight. Perhaps most players would now retreat the knight to b6 (which turns out to be safest). But instead of retreating, Euwe played 1. ... Ba4, an in-between move that counter-attacks the knight on e1.

That brings us to the puzzle position. Lasker found his own in-between move, **2. b4!**, when Black has two pieces under attack and can save only one. The game continued **2. ... Bxb4 3. Nc2!**, and the extra piece soon brought White victory.

Chapter 5

Finding the right plan

This chapter starts a section on middlegame stratgy. Chess is famously a game of *strategy*, a word synonymous with long-term planning. You've probably heard the expression "He's playing chess while his enemies are playing checkers." No offense to lovers of the king-me game, but the meaning is clear—chess players are the long-term planners. It takes everything you've already learned so far to understand chess strategy.

Strategy contrasts to tactics, which are short-term. If tactics are the hammer and nails of chess, strategy is the blueprint. But like any military commander, before a chess player can make a plan, he or she must evaluate the battlefield. Strategy begins with taking stock of the battle conditions and resources.

This chapter will give you the tools to make that evaluation, allowing you to make a fitting plan that establishes attainable objectives. These objectives will then suggest a choice of moves, called *candidate moves*, usually one to three possibilities, to implement that plan. The very last step in the process is choosing your move from among the candidates.

❝ All men can see the tactics whereby I conquer, but what none can see is the strategy out of which victory is evolved. ❞

66 The rules of strategy are few and simple. They may be learned in a week. 99

Masters associate strategy most with the middlegame. We're going to share with you the tools that masters use in that first step of forming a strategy—evaluation of the position on the board.

Six strategic tools

The method for any logical analysis requires breaking the whole into parts and assessing each part, then putting your evaluations together to get an overall conclusion. Evaluating a chess position follows the same logic. What are the parts we look at? You've already learned some of the key components.

King safety

The first question to ask yourself is "How safe is each king?" It's easy to understand that the safety of His Majesty trumps everything else. After all, if a player is checkmated, extra pawns and pieces make no difference. We list king safety here to give it emphasis, but will examine particulars in the next chapter, Attack and Defense.

Material advantage

This is perhaps the easiest component to assess, and you already know how to count up pawn and piece values (see page 16). If your king is safe, and you have a serious material advantage, you're most likely winning. In such a situation, the common strategy is to trade pieces and not pawns until you get to an overpowering endgame. If the king is safe, you're ahead material, and your opponent's king is unsafe, well, that's the trifecta. You can use the trade method or possibly use your extra material to force checkmate.

Tip Make the right trade

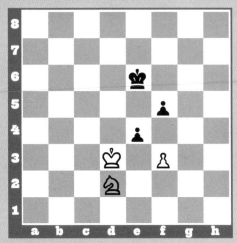

White to move

Never trade material thoughtlessly! In the position above, the "automatic" capture, 1. f3xe4?, would result in a hopelessly drawn position after 1. ... f5xe4 2. Nxe4, when White has insufficient material to checkmate. Instead 1. Nxe4! results in a won king and pawn endgame for White after 1. ... f5xe4 2. Kxe4!. White can force the pawn to its promotion square, making a queen and easily checkmating Black. (You'll learn just how to checkmate in the Endgame chapter.)

In positions that are more nearly equal, the following factors become important.

The center

You've learned the importance of the center, and even different schools of thought about dealing with it—occupy it and defend your fortifications, or entice the enemy to occupy it and harass that commitment. You've learned that a powerful center can stifle enemy plans before they can get started. You've learned as well that control of center enables the quick transference of your troops from one part of the board to another. Assessing who's better in the center and why is an important part of evaluation.

Development

This is yet another element that you're already familiar with. How many pieces on relevant squares does each side enjoy? Whose minor and major pieces are ready for sudden deployment to attack or defend? Does one player have better development? If the lead in development is big enough, it can even lead to a successful sacrifice of material for an attack on the king.

Mobility/space/ activity

These three strategic terms are closely related and a bit different from development. A player's pieces may be on good-looking squares— knights on f3 and c3 as White, for example—but unable to move safely from those squares. A position is referred to as cramped if a player doesn't have elbow room to reconfigure the pieces responsibly to a threat or opportunity. Such a player lacks mobility. On the other hand, if a player's pieces control many squares and have active chances to improve their positions and even to infiltrate the enemy's camp, that's an important plus.

Open lines

Rooks are happiest on open files, where they can exercise their great power from a distance. Just like other heavy artillery, rooks are sometimes a bit cumbersome to get into action and aren't well placed as mere defenders. They require a clear firing zone to be effective. Bishops can also be deadly on open diagonals, but as we've seen, are quicker to get into the fray—more like commandos than artillery.

In the middlegame, a rook loves to be on the seventh rank (the enemy's second rank), where it's always a danger. It can keep the opposing king cut off, attack pawns, and even threaten checkmate. In fact, the general rule is that getting your rook safely to the seventh rank is worth a pawn.

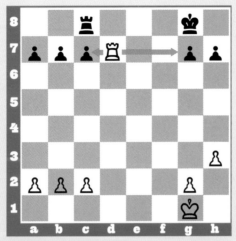

A hard-to-unseat rook on the seventh

In this position, White's rook is very annoying. Black's rook can't leave the protection of the c7-pawn, and Black's king must guard the g7-pawn.

Doubled rooks on the enemy's second rank are so strong that they are often called "blind pigs"—after their habit of gobbling up everything they touch.

Black has "blind pigs" and wins, no matter who is to move.

66 Beat the enemy in occupying the raised and sunny spots. 99

In the middlegame, the center is still important. But other parts of the board can become critical. Securing a fortified square on your opponent's side of the board can have much the same effect as combat troops occupying important territory behind enemy lines. And we'll see that the formation of your pawns—the foot soldiers of chess—can favor one type of minor piece over another.

Pawns, outposts, and minor pieces

Three centuries ago, the French musical composer and chess champion François-André Danican Philidor called pawns "the soul of chess." He was among the first to recognize that the platoon of privates in the trenches can form the shape of the battle.

The poor placement of pawns can create *weak squares* in your position, squares vulnerable to the occupation of enemy pieces. Your weak squares are your enemy's *strong squares*. When a player occupies a strong square with a piece, this establishes an outpost. Allowing an enemy *outpost* is fraught with danger.

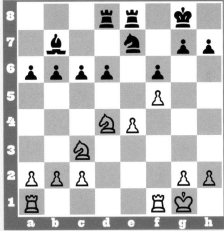

White plays 1. Ne6! with a dominating outpost.

Be careful with your pawns—after all, they can't move backward! (Notice that in the position above, Black would love to have a pawn on d7 or f7, controlling the e6-square.) Misplacing any other chessman can be corrected, with time as the only price you pay. But once moved, a pawn can never go home.

On their own, pawn formations can be weak, strong, or double-edged. But pawn structures are important also because they affect where enemy pieces can safely land. Taking pawn formations into consideration is very important in evaluating a position.

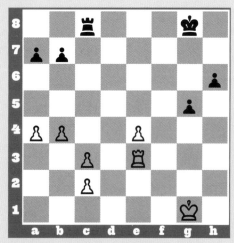

Examples of pawn formations

In the diagram above, White and Black have connected pawns on the a- and b-files. White has doubled pawns on the c-file, both of which are backward—you can see that Black's rook is well placed to threaten White's c-pawns. White has a passed pawn on the e-file, which is also an isolated pawn. Black has a protected passed pawn on g5 and a backward pawn, which is also a passed pawn, on h6.

Strong pawn formations
- **Connected pawns**—two or more pawns on adjacent files.
- **Passed pawn**—a pawn with no enemy pawns on files in front of or adjacent to it.
- **Protected passed pawn**—a passed pawn protected by a friendly pawn.

Weak pawn formations
- **Isolated pawns**—a pawn with no friendly pawns on adjacent files.
- **Doubled/tripled pawns**—two or three friendly pawns on the same file.
- **Backward pawns**—a pawn whose neighboring pawns have been pushed forward; backward pawns may be weak due to lack of protection by other pawns.

We should note that, although backward pawns don't have much to recommend themselves, there are times when both isolated pawns and doubled pawns can be contributors. For example, sometimes in the middlegame, having doubled pawns gives you a valuable open file, and sometimes the doubled pawns control key center squares. But avoid backward, isolated, and doubled pawns unless you have a specific reason to think they're a good tradeoff for an advantage you receive. Sometimes, as Bobby Fischer said, "You gotta give squares to get squares." Chess is about making choices.

Let's take the rooks off and rearrange the pawns a bit to illustrate another important idea—*one pawn restraining two.*

In the next diagram, if it's Black's turn, 1. ... b5! restrains both White's a- and c-pawns. With best play, Black would then win. If White is on move, 1. c4! pre-empts Black's restraining move. Then, with best play, it's a complicated draw.

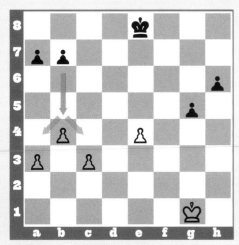

Black to move wins with 1. ... b5!.

Knight v bishop

Pawn formations can also be favorable or unfavorable for the knight or bishop. Although the values of knights and bishops are theoretically about equal, the two minor pieces could hardly be more different. A list of their major attributes shows the contrast:

Bishop	Knight
•Long range	•Short range
•Moves along the diagonal	•Jumps in an L-shaped pattern
•Restricted to only one color	•Alternates the color square it's on with every move

When an enemy knight and bishop confront each other, the terrain they find themselves in can change their relative values. Think of Napoleon's vaunted artillery mired in the mud at Waterloo, or the famous battle of Thermopylae, where a narrow pass allowed the Greeks to delay a Persian force many times their size.

Tip Opening a second front

Sometimes when you have an advantage, no matter how you hammer at an enemy weakness, your opponent will muster ways to defend. At those times, it can be effective to open up a second front—causing a second weakness. Your opponent then has to shift the defenders to meet the new attack. This demand can stretch the defence's resources to breaking point, especially if your army is more mobile and can shift the attacks quickly.

As Sun Tzu wrote: "*For should the enemy strengthen his vanguard, he will weaken his rear; should he strengthen his rear, he will weaken his vanguard.*"

The game Vassily Smyslov v Mikhail Tal (see page 82) is a good example of such a strategy in the endgame. The idea is also useful to know in the middlegame.

> 66 Water shapes its course according to the nature of the ground over which it flows; the soldier works out his victory in relation to the foe whom he is facing. 99

Chess games don't start with a middlegame terrain that favors one army's pieces over the other. The champion player adapts the army to the battleground that takes shape.

Master Games

Since pawn formations often determine the terrain, pawns frequently dictate whether the knight or bishop is better. The first game is a classic illustration of both weak and strong squares and a knight romping to victory over a bishop restricted by his friendly pawns.

On pages 82–83, Tal's bishop-over-knight masterpiece is as fine an effort as Fischer's knight-better-than-bishop brilliancy. But in both cases, the pawn formations determined which minor piece, in the hands of a champion, would prevail.

The exciting game on pages 84–85 shows the strategic tools discussed in this chapter working together in the hands of an attacking genius.

Good Knight, Mr Bolbochan!

American Bobby Fischer shows Argentinean champ Julio Bolbochan how to achieve a position in which the knight is superior to the bishop—and how to play it. Note how, throughout the game, Fischer uses tactics to secure a better and better position until Bolbochan is left with a hopeless game.

ROBERT JAMES FISCHER v JULIO
BOLBOCHAN
SICILIAN DEFENSE, STOCKHOLM
INTERZONAL, 1962

1. e4 c5 **2.** Nf3 d6 **3.** d4 cxd4
4. Nxd4 Nf6 **5.** Nc3 a6 **6.** h3
Nc6 **7.** g4 Nxd4 **8.** Qxd4 e5
9. Qd3 Be7 **10.** g5! Nd7 **11.** Be3
Nc5 **12.** Qd2 Be6 **13.** 0–0–0 0–0
14. f3 Rc8 **15.** Kb1 Nd7 **16.** h4
b5 **17.** Bh3 Bxh3 **18.** Rxh3 Nb6
19. Bxb6 Qxb6 **20.** Nd5

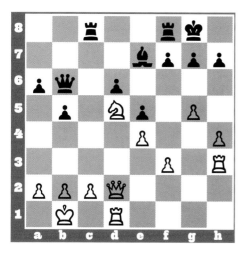

Fischer sinks his knight into the
weak square created by Black's
backward pawn. He even does it
with a tempo by attacking Black's
queen at the same time. So, in a
way, he gets a "free" move. Compare
the knight's dominating position to
the bishop's, blocked in by both
friendly and enemy pawns.

20. ... Qd8 **21.** f4
Not 21. Nxe7+? Qxe7 22. Qxd6?? Rfd8
when White is lost.

21. ... exf4 **22.** Qxf4 Qd7
23. Qf5 Rcd8
23. ... Rfd8? is no solution: 24. Qxd7
Rxd7 25.Nb6. Neither is 23...Qxf5? 24.
Nxe7+, using a different fork to wind
up a piece ahead.

24. Ra3! Qa7 **25.** Rc3 g6!
26. Qg4 Qd7 **27.** Qf3 Qe6
28. Rc7 Rde8 **29.** Nf4 Qe5
30. Rd5 Qh8 **31.** a3 h6
32. gxh6 Qxh6 **33.** h5 Bg5
34. hxg6! fxg6 **35.** Qb3!

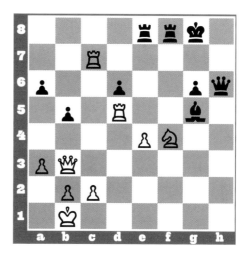

35. ... Rxf4
Black finally gets to capture the
knight that Fischer has used to shred
Black's position—but it does
Bolbochan no good now. If 35. ...
Bxf4, White wins with 36. Rh5+. It also
did no good to avoid the upcoming
discovered check with 35. ... Kh8:
36. Nxg6+ Qxg6 37. Rxg5 Rf1+ (or
37. ... Qxg5 38. Qh3, and it's mate
in two) 38. Ka2 Qxg5 39. Qh3+ Kg8
40. Qxf1.

36. Re5+! **36.** Kf8 **37.** Rxe8+
It's certain checkmate: 37. ... Kxe8
38.Qe6+ Kf8 39. Qc8#.

66 All we need do is to attack some other place that he will be obliged to relieve. 99

A Bishop Stands Tal

Two former World Champions contest this endgame classic. Russian Vassily Smyslov reigned from 1957 to 1958. Latvian Mikhail Tal held the world title from 1960 to 1961. Besides showing a superior bishop over a knight, their famous endgame also illustrates the idea of the second front. A beleaguered player may be able to hold the fort against one weakness, but may well collapse when a second front is opened.

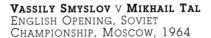

VASSILY SMYSLOV V **MIKHAIL TAL**
ENGLISH OPENING, SOVIET
CHAMPIONSHIP, MOSCOW, 1964

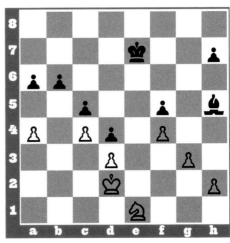

Black to move

Watch how Tal uses his bishop to draw White's king to the defense of his a-pawn, then switches the action to the kingside. Ultimately, the short-range knight is at too much of a disadvantage. White can't defend on two widely separate fronts.

35. ... a5!
Tal immobilizes the isolated pawn on a4 as a target.

36. Kc2 Be8 **37.** Kb3 Bc6
38. Ka3 Kf6 **39.** Kb3 Kg6
40. Ka3 Kh5 **41.** h3 Kg6
42. Kb3 Kg7 **43.** Ka3 Kf6
44. Kb3 Be8! **45.** Ng2 Bh5
46. Kc2 Be2 **47.** Ne1 Bf1
48. Nf3

In trying to keep things even on the kingside, White's short-hopping knight has been diverted out of range of the queenside weakling on a4.

53. Kc1 Bg2

Black could capture the a-pawn immediately, but he's enjoying winning on both wings!

54. Kd2 Kh5 **55.** Ne6

If 55. Ke2, Black plays 55. ... Kg4 56. Kf2 Bc6 57. Nf7 Bxa4 58. Nh6+ Kh5 59. Nxf5 Bd7 60. Nd6 a4 61. Ne4 a3 62. Nd2 Ba4. Black will queen the a-pawn. The line again shows up the advantage of the long-range bishop with pawns on both sides of the board.

55. ... Kg4 **56.** Nc7 Bc6
57. Nd5 Kxg3 **58.** Ne7 Bd7
59. Nd5 Bxa4 **60.** Nxb6 Be8
61. Nd5 Kf3 **62.** Nc7 Bc6
63. Ne6 a4 **64.** Nxc5 a3
65. Nb3 a2 **66.** Kc1 Kxf4
67. Kb2 Ke3 **68.** Na5 Be8
69. c5 f4 **70.** c6 Bxc6 **71.** Nxc6 f3 **72.** Ne5 f2 White resigns

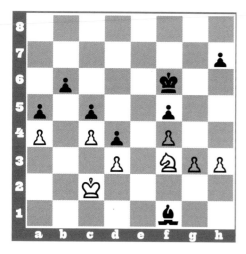

48. ... Bxh3

Tal lops off the underpinnings of White's kingside.

49. Ng5 Bg2 **50.** Nxh7+ Kg7
51. Ng5 Kg6 **52.** Kd2 Bc6

73. Ng4+ Ke2 74. Nxf2 Kxf2 75. Kxa2 Ke2 76. Kb1 Kxd3 77. Kc1 Ke2 and Black's pawn marches to its coronation.

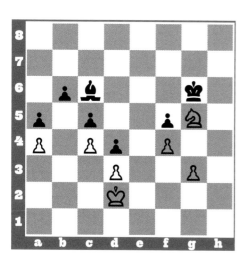

> ## 66 It was only when he intended a surprise, or when a rapid retreat was imperative, that he sacrificed everything for speed. 99

Take my pawns, please!

Walter Browne was one of the most aggressive and imaginative grandmasters of his generation. Here he uses an open center and an overwhelming lead in development to establish an advantage in space and mobility that makes Black's material gains irrelevant. Although Browne's opponent in this game, Argentinean grandmaster Miguel Quinteros, was one of the world's elite players, in this instance he succumbed to pure material greed, falling far behind in development and, ultimately, failing to keep his king safe.

WALTER BROWNE V **MIGUEL QUINTEROS**
SICILIAN DEFENSE, HOOGOVENS WIJK
AAN ZEE, 1974

**1. e4 c5 2. Nf3 d6 3. Bb5+ Bd7
4. Bxd7+ Qxd7 5. c4 Qg4?!**
Too greedy! Black ignores development to double-attack pawns on e4 and g2.

**6. 0–0 Qxe4 7. d4 cxd4
8. Re1 Qc6?!**
8. ... Qg4 would slow White's attack.

9. Nxd4 Qxc4?

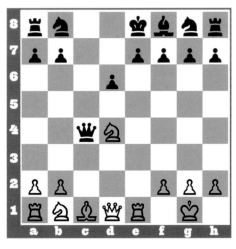

Black takes pawn-snatching to suicidal extremes, ignoring his development and leaving his king unsafe in the center for too long. White is already castled, with a rook on the semi-open e-file vis-à-vis the enemy king, and a centralized knight.

10. Na3

Developing while harassing Black's queen—the knight will move to a better square soon.

10. ... Qc8 11. Bf4

White threatens 12. Bxd6, since the pawn on e7 is pinned by the rook.

11. ... Qd7 12. Nab5

White renews the threat on d6.

12. ... e5

The double attack on White's bishop and knight is an empty threat, since the e-pawn remains pinned to the king.

13. Bxe5!

White is so far ahead in development that he can sacrifice a piece to expose the black king.

13. ... dxe5 14. Rxe5+ Be7

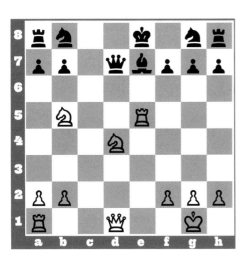

15. Rd5! Qc8

If 15. ... Qxd5, then 16. Nc7+ wins the queen with a fork.

16. Nf5

The biggest threat isn't 17. Nxg7+. It's 17. Nbd6+ Bxd6 18. Nxd6+, forking Black's king and queen.

16. ... Kf8 17. Nxe7 Kxe7

Black's king is in the center with no cover, vulnerable to White's artillery. If instead 17. ... Nxe7, then 18. Rd8+ Qxd8 19. Qxd8 checkmate.

18. Re5+! Black resigns.

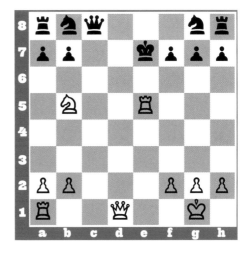

Quinteros foresees his doom and calls it quits—for example: 18. ... Kf8 19. Qd6+ Ne7 20. Qxe7+ Kg8 21. Qe8+ Qxe8 22. Rxe8#.

66 Hence that general is skillful in attack whose opponent does not know what to defend; and he is skillful in defense whose opponent does not know what to attack. 99

Chapter 6

Attack and defense

Attack against an enemy king is the most exciting concept in chess. It harkens back in miniature to the epic battles of Napoleon, Caesar, Alexander the Great, and, of course, Sun Tzu. A "mating attack" is the action-adventure movie of the chessboard. Many chess players relish the role of a general directing such an offensive. Some players, we should also note, are more comfortable in the defensive role, delighting in thwarting the opponent's bold thrusts. A complete chess player can both attack and defend.

Sun Tzu's chapter-opening quote tells us that preparation makes the victor. It's true in war and in chess. It's true in the sense that chess players need to prepare by learning important strategic ideas in their general training. And it's true in the sense that in a given chess game, the piling up of advantages must precede a successful attack. Chess is a logical game, so why should we expect to win without first getting a better position?

> **66** **Rapidity is the essence of war. Take advantage of the enemy's unreadiness, make your way by unexpected routes, and attack unguarded spots. 99**

The first World Champion, Wilhelm Steinitz, taught us that we cannot expect our attacks to succeed unless we have first accumulated relevant advantages. Moreover, he told us that if we have such an advantage and do not launch an attack, we will surely fritter away that advantage.

Attacks on the uncastled king

The strategic ideas that were discussed on pages 74–79 come together to guide you in attack and defense. Open lines, both files and diagonals, become highways for the attacking forces. Outposts, especially entrenched knights, become bastions of the assault. Center formations, as well as center thrusts and counter-thrusts, can promote attack or even mount a counter-offensive. Whenever an attack succeeds, of course, the defender has made fatal mistakes. The mistakes may have been made during the attack or even before the attack was launched—by weakening the position so much that no defense would succeed.

Attacks on the enemy king can be usefully divided into three situations:

- Attacks on the uncastled king.
- Attacks on the castled king when both players have castled kingside.
- Attacks when the players have castled on opposite sides. (Games in which both players castle queenside are rare.)

You've learned that king safety is a chess player's number one priority. You must be alert at each move for threats to your king. You know that you should castle early, whisking your king off the center files to a safer, better-guarded position. When a king is suddenly caught in the center (and here we mean along the center files, not the very center of the board), the attack can be quickly overwhelming.

When an attack on the uncastled king is called for, you should:

- Prevent the enemy king from escaping the center;
- Develop quickly and involve as many pieces in the attack as possible;
- Open lines—diagonals and central files.

Usually we think of Black being the victim, since White has the advantage of the first move, but that doesn't have to be the case. Take a look at the following miniature:

1. d4 Nf6 2. Nd2 e5 3. dxe5 Ng4 4. h3?? Ne3! 5. fxe3 Qh4+ 6. g3 Qxg3#

Remember that, before castling, a frequent weak point is f7 (for Black) and f2 (for White). Here's a famous sequence that's routed many an unwary player:

1. e4 e5 2. d4 exd4 3. c3 dxc3 4. Nxc3 Nc6 5. Bc4 Be7 6. Qd5

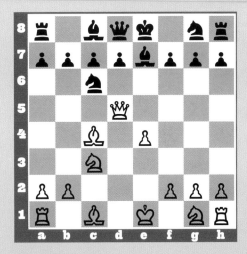

With the threat of a quick checkmate on f7, Black's only reasonable move is **6. ... Nh6**, but after **7. Bxh6**, it's already hopeless for Black, who blocked the coordination of the defense with 5. ... Be7, a move that ignored the center. (Notice that if the bishop wasn't on e7, Black's queen could move to that square to defend f7. Also note that a knight on f6 would have prevented White's queen from occupying d5.)

White's second move was passive, putting the knight on an unaggressive square and blocking in the dark-squared bishop. But the fourth move was criminal, ignoring development altogether and weakening the d1–h4 diagonal.

Not all attacks against the uncastled king are so quick and simple, of course. The Magerramov–Kasparov game on pages 95–97 is an example of a brilliant and methodical attack that proved successful—for Black.

66 Appear at points that the enemy must hasten to defend; march swiftly to places where you are not expected. 99

In ancient battles and on the chessboard, a king is generally kept in safety. For if he is captured or killed, his forces are defeated. But sometimes when a king thinks he's safely protected, he falls victim to an unforeseen attack. It happened in the Battle of Poitiers in 1356 and it happened in the game Palatnik–Geller in 1980.

Attacks on the castled king

A king in a castled position is generally much safer than a king still on the center files. But just because you are castled does not mean your king is automatically safe! King safety is always the highest priority. You should be concerned with it on every move.

After castling kingside, a frequent weak point is h7. Examine the following position from a game between famous grandmasters. It's Black to move. What would you do?

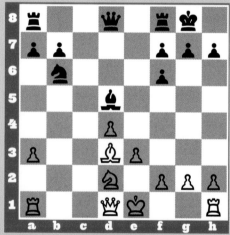

Palatnik–Geller, Rostov, USSR 1980. Black to move.

Black (a world-class grandmaster) feels his own kingside is solid. He sees a chance to win a pawn and quash White's kingside castling option.

1. ... Bxg2?? 2. Rg1 Bc6 3. Rxg7+!
White resigns.

This rook sacrifice must have come as a shock, but it wins by force and is perfectly logical. Black almost forced White to install his heavy artillery where it had a direct shot at the enemy king, on the g-file. Black resigned here because he saw what was coming: 3. ... Kxg7 4. Qg4+ 4. Kh8 5. Qf5.

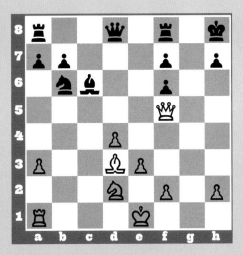

White used a time-gaining check on g4 to assemble an unstoppable battery of bishop and queen. No matter what Black does, he'll be checkmated when White's queen goes to h7. Once again, if Black had maintained a defensive knight on f6, it would have guarded both g4 and the sensitive h7.

Removing a key defender

Let's look at a classic grandmaster game in which Black did have a defending knight posted on the recommended f6 square, but made weakening moves that allowed White to concentrate on removing the key defender—an important attacking concept.

Capablanca–Levenfish, Moscow, 1935. After 19. ... h6

Black has just pushed his h-pawn to attack White's bishop on g5, which is pinning the f6-knight to Black's queen, a very common tactic. But White sees that the knight on f6 is the linchpin of Black's defenses, the key defender, and that opening the h-file with ... hxg5 would be a fatal mistake.

20. Ng4!
Now nothing can stave off the mating attack.

20. ... Be7
If 20. ... hxg5?, then 21. Nxf6+ gxf6 22. Qh7#.

21. Bxf6 gxf6

If instead Black recaptures with
21. ... Bxf6 (see analysis diagram,
below right), White plays 22. Nxh6+
gxh6 23. Qxh6 Re8 24. Bh7+ Kh8 25.
Bg6+ Kg8 26. Qh7+ Kf8 27. Qxf7#—a
mating pattern you've learned.

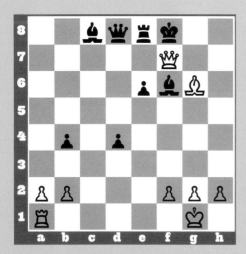

22. Nxh6+ Kg7 23. Qg4+ Kh8

If 23. ... Kxh6, then 24. Qh4+ Kg7
25. Qh7#.

24. Qh5 Kg7

If 24. ... f5 25. Nxf5+ Kg8 26. Nxe7+
Qxe7 27. Qh7#.

25. Nxf7 Rh8 26. Qg6+ Black resigns.

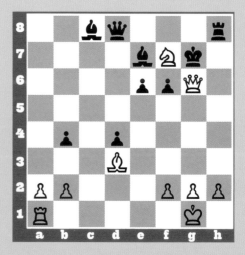

Black will not only lose his rook,
he will be checkmated by force:
26. ... Kf8 27. Nxh8 Qe8 28. Qh6+
Kg8 29. Qh7+ Kf8 30. Ng6+ Qxg6
31. Bxg6, and now after any move
by Black (e.g. 31. ... Bd7) 32. Qf7#.

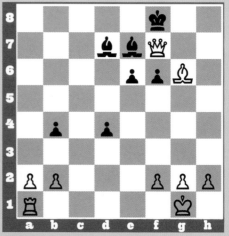

Analysis diagram after 32. Qf7#

Kamsky–Shankland (see pages
99–101) is a complete grandmaster
game that illustrates an exciting
attack on the castled king.

66 In battle there are not more than two methods of attack—the direct and the indirect; yet these two in combination give rise to an endless series of maneuvers. 99

In the following example we take a look at an attack on a king castled on the opposite side of the chessboard. In Razuvaev–Kapengut, Black is able to fend off White's attempt to create open files by means of a pawn storm. But indirect methods along the opened diagonals culminate in a surprising queen sacrifice that nets overwhelming material.

Attacks with opposite-side castling

The first rule of attack when kings are castled on opposite sides is that whoever is first to breach the enemy's defenses normally wins. "Get there firstest with the mostest"— as Confederate general Nathan Forrest put it. To put it in our own words, we'd say that initiative and superior forces in the area of the attack are indicators of success.

Since a typically successful defensive stratagem often calls for countering a wing attack with a counter in the center, the attacker wants a locked center, or a center that is firmly under control, to prevent such diversions.

Pawn storms

When the kings are castled on opposite wings, pawn storms are the most common attacking plan. Pawn storms are simply the pushing of the attacker's pawns toward the enemy's king position. Since the attacker's king is not ensconced behind these pawns, it is not endangered by this tactic. The attacker often doesn't mind if these hara-kiri pawns are captured, because then open lines are produced in front of the enemy king position. Pawn storms are successful when the defender has somehow weakened or has been forced to weaken the pawns in front of the king.

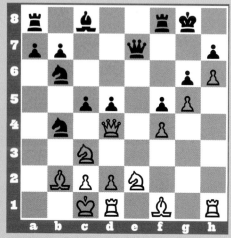

Razuvaev–Kapengut, 1970. After
19. ... c5

We can see that White has pushed a
storm of pawns against Black's king,
and that Black has avoided opening
files by avoiding capturing any of
the oncoming missiles. But he did
create an open diagonal to the
heart of his defensive bunker! It's
true, however, that White's bishop on
b2 appears to be obstructed by its
own pieces.

20. Qh8+!
This bolt-from-the-blue queen
sacrifice creates a discovered check
on the long diagonal.

**20. ... Kxh8 21. Nxd5+ Kg8
22. Nxe7+ Kf7 23. Nxc8 Black
resigns.**
Black's a piece down without
compensation. Sometimes a
kingside attack converts itself into a
substantial win of material.

The Karpov–Korchnoi game on
pages 103–104 illustrates an
exemplary attack when the kings
are castled on opposite wings.

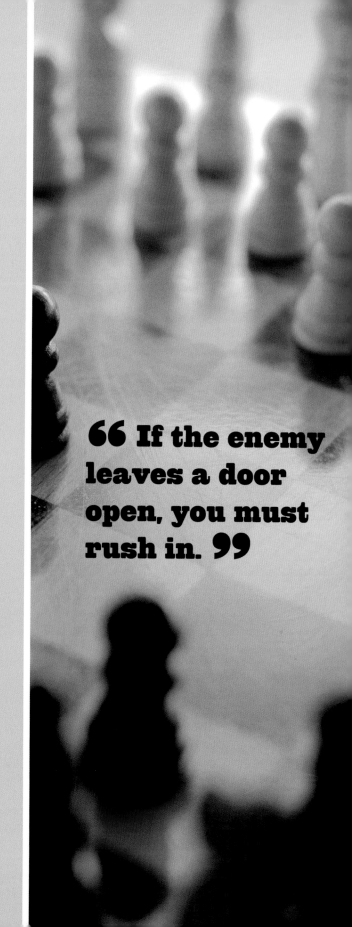

66 If the enemy
leaves a door
open, you must
rush in. **99**

Master games

Attacking the king in the center

Although these kinds of attacks are rare in today's master play, because both sides know the importance of development and castling early, a game can sometimes still explode like a landmine in an incautious defender's face.

Garry Kasparov of the Soviet Union was World Champion from 1985 to 2000. He's one of three or four players in the history of the game who are often cited as the best of all time. His opponent, a talented champion from Azerbaijan, went on to earn his grandmaster title and become champion of the Soviet Union. Perhaps he benefitted from the lesson Kasparov gave him in this encounter.

ELMAR MAGERRAMOV V GM GARRY KASPAROV
QUEEN'S GAMBIT DECLINED,
TARTAKOWER VARIATION
BAKU, 1977

1. Nf3 Nf6 2. d4 e6 3. c4 d5 4. Nc3 Be7 5. Bg5 0–0 6. e3

The opening has transposed into a Queen's Gambit Declined, Tartakower Variation, which develops Black's "problem" c8-bishop, hemmed in by the e6-pawn, by fianchettoing it on b7.

6. ... h6 7. Bh4 b6 8. Qb3 Bb7 9. Bxf6 Bxf6 10. cxd5 exd5 11. Rd1 c5! 12. dxc5 Nd7 13. c6!?

After 13. cxb6 Nc5 14. Qc2 axb6, Black has played a gambit and achieved satisfactory compensation for the pawn with his open lines and piece activity. White's game move is an attempt to slow Black's attack.

continued on next page

13. ... Bxc6 14. Nd4?!

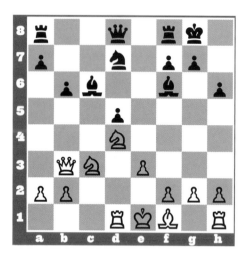

The follow-up idea to White's last move, attacking the bishop on c6. But Black sees how to gain time and retain the bishop that aims at the kingside!

If 14. Nxd5!? Nc5 15. Nxf6+ Qxf6, Black would once again have plenty of piece activity and a lead in development to offset his pawn deficit.

14. ... Bxd4! 15. Rxd4?!

If instead 15. exd4, 15. ... Qg5 16. g3 Rfe8+ 17. Be2. Now 17. ... Qg4! keeps White from castling and shows up the weakness of his light squares: 18. h3 Qf3.

15. ... Nc5! 16. Qd1 Ne6!
17. Rd2 d4! 18. exd4 Re8 19. f3

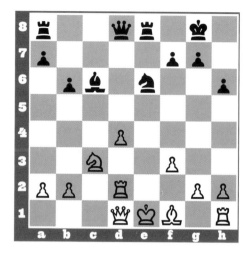

Of course, if 19.Be2, then ... Bxg2.

If you're wondering about the possibility of 19. d5, here's a long and convincing analysis that the great chess commander Kasparov must have had in mind. It begins with a discovered check: 19. ... Nf4+ 20. Be2 Nxg2+ 21. Kf1 Bd7! 22. h4 (not 22. Kxg2? Qg5+ 23. Bh3+ 24. Ke1 Qg2 25. Rd4 Qxh1+ 26. Kd2 Qxh2, and Black is winning because of his extra material and the continuing weakness of the white king) 22. ... Nf4 23. Bg4 Bxg4 24. Qxg4 Qf6. Black remains on top because of the fragile state of White's king.

After the game move 19. f3, it's clear that White will pay the price of keeping his king in the center too long.

19. ... Bxf3!! 20. gxf3 Qh4+
21. Rf2 Nxd4+ 22. Be2 Nxf3+
23. Kf1 Qh3+

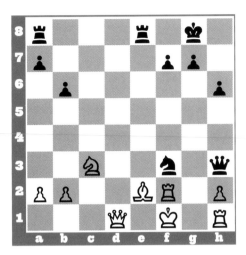

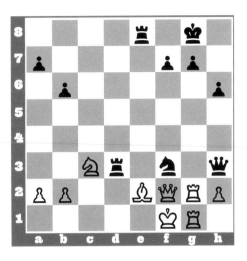

**24. Rg2 Nh4 25. Rhg1 Rad8
26. Qe1**

28. Rh1
Other defensive tries also fail: 28.
Nb5 Rd1+ 29. Bxd1 Nxh2#; or 28. Qg3
Nd2+! 29. Ke1 Rxg3 30. Rxg3 Nf3+ 31.
Kf2 Nxg1! 32. Rxh3 Nxh3+; or 28. Bxd3
Nxh2#.

28. ... Rde3! 29. Rhg1
29. Bxf3 Rxf3 30. Qxf3 Qxf3+ 31. Kg1
Re1#

29. ... Kh8 30. Rh1

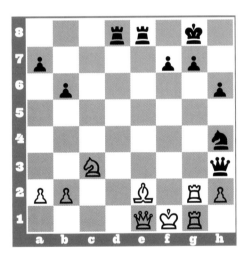

White could try 26. Qa4, but Black
then has 26. ... Nf5! 27. Qf4 Rd4!
28. Qf3 (28. Qf2 Rd2!) 28. ... Ne3+ 29.
Kf2 Qh4+ 30. Qg3 Qf6+ 31. Bf3 Rd2+
32. Ke1 Rxg2! 33. Rxg2 Nf5+, winning
the queen with a discovered check.

26. ... Rd3!
Threatening 27. ... Rf3#!

27. Qf2 Nf3!

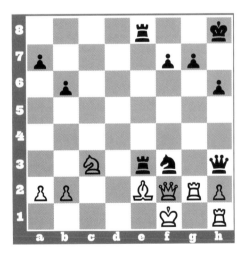

30. ... b5!! White resigns
White's army is completely pinned
down, and he can't stop the coming
pawn attack that will dislocate his
knight, leaving his bishop
defenseless: 31. a3 a5 32. Rhg1 b4 33.
axb4 axb4 34. Nd1 Rxe2.

66 You may advance and be absolutely irresistible if you make for the enemy's weak points. 99

Attacking the kingside: Greek Sacrifice

The Greeks famously sacked Troy by appearing to abandon their offensive and offering a huge wooden "Trojan Horse" outside the city walls. Once the celebrating Trojans brought in the apparent tribute and night fell, a small band of Greeks led by Odysseus came out from hiding inside the horse and opened the gates for the rest of the Greek army, which massacred the Trojans.

On the chessboard, the "Greek gift" doesn't begin with the sacrifice of a knight, our chessboard horse. Instead, a bishop is offered.

In this chapter you've learned that the weakest point of a castled king's position is often h7 (or h2). The following game is an example of the Greek Sacrifice, when White plays Bxh7+. It's one of the most common sacrifices once Black has castled.

Unlike the incautious Trojans, Black normally has little choice about whether to accept the "free" bishop and can only try to find the best defensive moves, hoping the sacrifice won't quite work. The follow-up for White normally requires White to place a knight on g5 and a rook on the e-file.

GATA KAMSKY v **SAM SHANKLAND**, STURBRIDGE, MASSACHUSETTS, 2014

Gata Kamsky was a Soviet chess prodigy who defected to the USA in 1989 when he was 14. He went on to earn an unsuccessful challenge match against World Champion Anatoly Karpov in 1996 and to win four US Championships. Sam Shankland became a grandmaster at 19. Six months after this game, he earned a gold medal for his performance at the chess Olympiad in Norway, where Kamsky was a teammate.

1. d4 Nf6 2. Bf4 d5 3. e3 e6 4. Nd2 c5 5. c3 Nc6 6. Ngf3 Bd6 7. Bg3 0–0 8. Bd3 Qe7 9. Ne5 Nd7 10. Nxd7 Bxd7

10. ... Qxd7 would have avoided a successful Greek gift. We will see later why.

11. Bxd6 Qxd6 12. dxc5

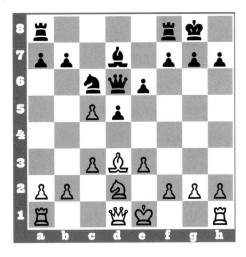

After this capture, White has an advantage, at least temporarily enjoying an extra pawn, because ...

12. ... Qxc5??

... is a serious mistake. None of Black's active pieces now protect the space in front of his king. 12. ... Qe7 or 12. ... Qc7 was necessary.

continued on next page

13. Bxh7+!

The Greek Sacrifice! Co-author Grandmaster Moradiabadi has won three games in this exact position after playing this move.

13. ... Kxh7 14. Qh5+ Kg8

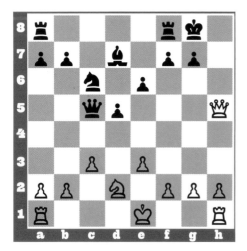

Stop for a moment before going on. You know that in order to attack successfully, White must rally more of his pieces to the kingside. By herself, the queen can't prevail. What's the move?

15. Ne4!

A nice tactic, foreseen by Kamsky. The knight takes advantage of the pinned d5-pawn and heads for the kingside, gaining a tempo by attacking Black's queen on the way!

15. ... Qc4

15. ... g6 does not work: 16. Nxc5 gxh5 17. Nxd7 Rfd8 18. Nf6+ Kg7 19. Nxh5+, and White would be two pawns up.

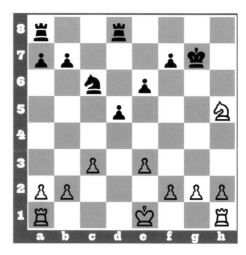

Now we can see the difference Black could have made with a better decision when he played 10. ... Bxd7. Had he played 10. ... Qxd7 instead, after White's 15. Ne4, 15. ... g6 would work, since White would not have the option of taking on c5 because there is no bishop on d7! The game would be equal: 10. ... Qxd7 11. Bxd6 Qxd6 12. dxc5 Qxc5 13. Bxh7+ Kxh7 14. Qh5+ Kg8 15. Ne4 g6 16. Qg5 (with the bishop no longer on d7 White cannot regain the piece by 16. Nxc5 etc.) Qa5 17. Nf6+ Kg7 18. Nh5+ Kh7 19. Nf6+ Kg7, with a draw by perpetual check.

16. Ng5

White threatens mate in one on h7.

16. ... Rfd8 17. Qxf7+ Kh8 18. Qh5+ Kg8

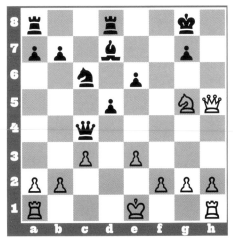

Analysis diagram after 19. Nxh5+

So, with queen and knight around the Black king and Black's pieces astray, White can draw by repeating the position. But is that why he sacrificed his bishop?

19. Rd1!
No! White brings reinforcements into the game.

19. ... e5 20. Qf7+ Kh8 21. e4
The d5-pawn is again pinned against the queen—this time on the diagonal! The black queen is completely cut off and a bad end looms for her king.

21. ... Ne7
Black tries giving back his extra piece. After 21. ... Rac8 22. Qh5+ Kg8 23. Rxd5, the mating net would then be drawn tight—for example: 23. ... Qxa2 would allow mate in four with 24. Qh7+ Kf8 25. Qh8+ Ke7 26. Qxg7+ Ke8 27. Qf7#.

22. Qxe7 Bb5
Black threatens checkmate on e2, but that bravado is easily thwarted.

**23. Rd2 Qxa2 24. Qf7 Qa1+
25. Rd1 Qxb2 26. Qh5+ Kg8
27. Qh7+ Kf8 28. Qh8+ Ke7
29. Qxg7+ Kd6 30. Rxd5+ Kc6
31. Qf6+ Black resigns.**

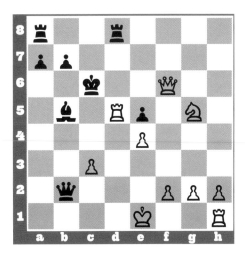

One sample denouement: 31. ... Kc7 32. Ne6+ Kc6 33. Nc5+ Kc7 34. Qe7+ Rd7 35. Rxd7+ Bxd7 36. Ne6+ Kc6 37. Qc5#.

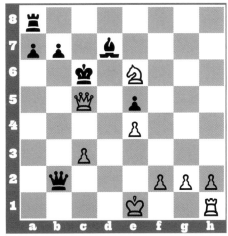

Analysis diagram after 37. Qc5

A beautiful outcome of the Greek Sacrifice, Bxh7+. Black's kingside defensive pawns have been annihilated, His Majesty stalked to the queenside and checkmated with queen and knight.

66 By persistently hanging on the enemy's flank, we shall succeed in the long run in killing the commander in chief—a vital act in war. 99

Opposite-side castling

The winner of this cutthroat contest, Russian Anatoly Karpov, became World Champion when Bobby Fischer refused to defend his crown. But Karpov proved himself worthy by going on to amass one of the most impressive winning records of any player. You'll appreciate White's technical attacking skills even more when you realize that his opponent, Victor Korchnoi, also of Russia, was one of the best defenders of all time.

Karpov lets loose a pawn storm once he knows that the opponent's king will be castling on the opposite side from his own. His attack gets fired up first and Black never gets anything serious going on the queenside, suffering a rare, crushing defensive debacle.

ANATOLY KARPOV V **VICTOR KORCHNOI**
SICILIAN DEFENSE, DRAGON VARIATION
WORLD CHAMPIONSHIP CANDIDATES
FINAL, MOSCOW, 1974

**1. e4 c5 2. Nf3 d6 3. d4 cxd4
4. Nxd4 Nf6 5. Nc3 g6**
Black signals that the Sicilian
variation he wants to play is the
Dragon, a double-edged and
dynamic opening.

**6. Be3 Bg7 7. f3 Nc6 8. Qd2
0–0 9. Bc4**

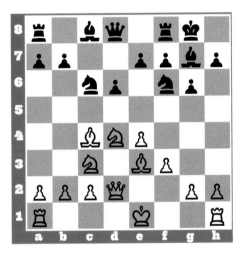

This dangerous White formation is
called the Yugoslav Attack and has
claimed many casualties of war of
all strengths. Theoretically, the
position is probably equal, but the
nearly "automatic" attacking moves
that White can play require great
defensive and counter-attacking
technique on Black's part.

9. ... Bd7 10. h4

White wastes no time in starting to
pry open the h-file. He's decided to
castle long. With kings on opposite
sides, victory usually belongs to the
side whose attack breaks through
first. Pawns don't count for much—in
fact, White would love for his h-pawn
to simply disappear, giving his rook
direct aim at h7.

**10. ... Rc8 11. Bb3 Ne5
12. 0–0–0 Nc4 13. Bxc4 Rxc4
14. h5 Nxh5 15. g4 Nf6
16. Nde2 Qa5 17. Bh6**
White plays a standard maneuver to
trade off Black's fianchettoed bishop,
weakening the dark squares around
Black's king and depriving him of a
piece that could be an effective
counter-attacker, aimed as it is
against the queenside.

17. ... Bxh6
17. ... Rfc8 18. Bxg7 Kxg7 19. Qh6+
Kg8 20. Rd5 also leaves White
somewhat better.

18. Qxh6

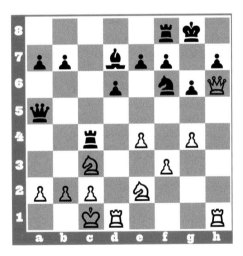

Notice now that Black's knight on f6
is the only reason White can't play
Qxh7#.

continued on next page

18. ... **Rfc8 19. Rd3 R4c5**
20. g5 Rxg5

If Black tries 20. ... Nh5, 21. Nf4 will get rid of the knight-blockader and open the h-file again. White would have a winning attack.

21. Rd5 Rxd5

Not 21. ... Nxd5?? 22. Qxh7+ Kf8 23. Qh8#.

22. Nxd5 Re8 23. Nef4 Bc6
24. e5! Bxd5 25. exf6 exf6 26.
Qxh7+ Kf8 27. Qh8+ Black
resigns.

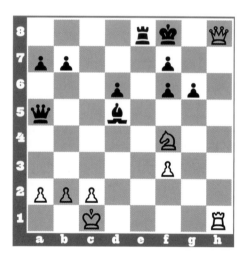

Black loses his rook: 27. ... Ke7 28. Nxd5+ This exchange deflects the black queen from its control of e1. 28...Qxd5 29.Re1+.

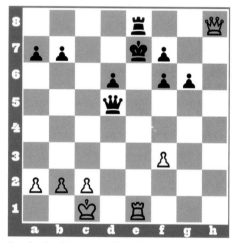

Analysis diagram after 29. Re1+

A nice finishing tactic: the black rook is *skewered* and will be double-attacked and captured after Black's king moves.

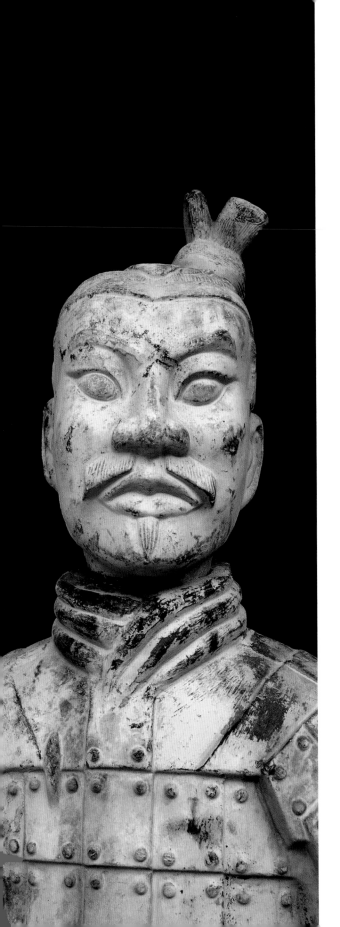

Practice puzzles

Apply what you've learned about strategy to evaluate each of the following positions before deciding on a move. You're not looking to find moves all the way to checkmate or, in some cases, even to an overwhelming position. Find the right plan called for by the position and the moves that initiate it. Read the explanations on the following pages carefully. We give you game citations so that, if you are interested, you can find the complete games online.

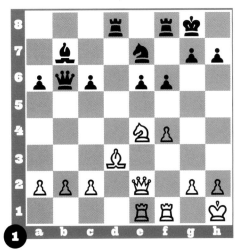

1

White to move

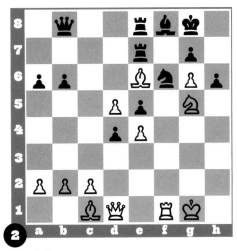

2

Black to move

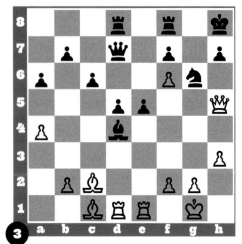

3 White to move

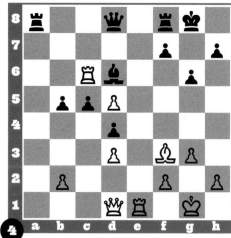

4 White to move

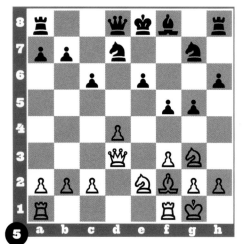

5 White to move

6 White to move

Solutions to puzzles on previous pages

1. Discovering a weakness

White assesses the position and sees that e6 is obviously weak, that the queen + rook battery will be powerful on the e-file, and that the bishop will dominate the kingside light squares. In addition, White takes careful note that Black's queen and blocked-in bishop are not well placed to defend the black king.

1. Ng5! fxg5 (Black has little choice: the knight moved with double attack *and* discovered attack) **2. Qe6+ Rf7 3. fxg5** (opening up the f-file to double attack the pinned black rook on f7) **3. ... Rdf8 4. Bc4.** Black will lose lots of material. (White actually has a forced mate in eight, but can win in other ways without having to look that far ahead.)

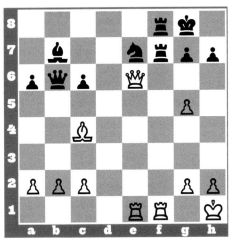

After 4. Bc4

If, on move 2, Black had chosen 2. ... Kh8, then 3. Qxe7 gxf4 4. Qd4+ g6 5. Qe5+ Kg8. 6. Bc4+, and Black is in more or less the same fix. That's the way the actual game—Grandelius–Pulvett, Reykjavik, 2015—went.

2. Returning material

This one's an excellent example of defensive technique. White has sacrificed an Exchange and a pawn to establish a *threatening outpost* on e6. Black takes stock of what White's position would be without the strongpoint and finds the only adequate move.

1. ... Rxe6! 2. Nxe6 Rxe6! 3. dxe6 Qe8!. Black has returned material (often the right defensive choice) to stymie White's attack. Black will own two pawns for the Exchange, in a position where White's king is wide open.

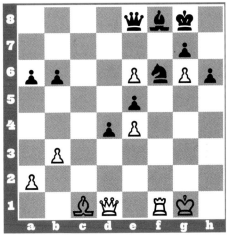

After 3. ... Qe8

The game is Gurevich–Schmaltz, Porz-Baden Oos, 2004. White, frustrated by the failure of his attacking scheme, made desperate choices and lost.

Solutions to puzzles on previous pages

3. Blasting open the e-file

Evaluate: Black is missing a kingside pawn-defender, and White has a dangerous pawn on f6, which can be used to support an invading white piece. White's bishops both strike ominously at Black's kingside—the fact that they are far away doesn't matter. White's rook artillery is centrally located, and the powerful queen is breathing down the black king's neck. All this allows White to end the battle with a few master strokes.

1. Rxd4! exd4 2. Re7! Qd6 (If **2. ... Nxe7 3. Qxh7#**) **3. Bxg6!**. White will checkmate Black in, at most, three moves—work this one out on your own too.

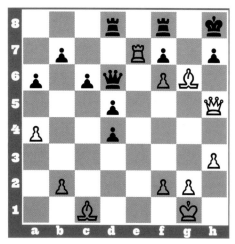

After 3. Bxg6!

The position is from Hansen–Tjomsland, Reykjavik, 2015.

4. March of the h-pawn

Black has just played ... g6, creating a target in front of the king at a time when White's pieces dominate the board. Co-author Grandmaster Moradiabadi seizes the opportunity to attack along the h-file.

1. Kg2! (preparing the attack)
1. ... Qb8 2. h4! Rd8 3. h5 Ra2 4. Qc1 (combining attack and defense)
4. ... Bf8 5. hxg6 hxg6 6. Qg5.

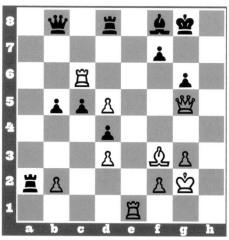

After 6. Qg5

The threats along the h-file (after Rh1) and against g6 are overwhelming. If 6. ... Rd6, either 7. Rh1 with an attack down the h-file, or 7. Qe5, pinning, gives White an advantage. Moradiabadi won in a few more moves. The game is Moradiabadi–Sarkar, Asheville, North Carolina, 2015.

5. Backward and weak

This is an example of a king, with a disorganized army, stuck in the center. Although the position is somewhat closed, Black's lack of development leads White to seize the opportunity for a quick breakthrough.

1. d5! cxd5 2. Nd4 Nc5 3. Qe2. In such a position, Black will come to no good. The knight on g7 sits on a terrible square, and the backward pawn on e6 is weak and pinned. White threatens to capture on f5 with either knight.

6. Exchange sacrifice

Here's another instructive defensive reaction. White, who has just played 1. g5, is hopeful about his kingside pawn storm. But Black, a World Champion, turns White's attempted attack into a debacle in a few deft moves. He sees that a thematic Exchange sacrifice defangs White's center and gives Black control of the long light diagonal.

1. ... Rxc3! 2. bxc3 Nxe4 3. Qg4 Qc8

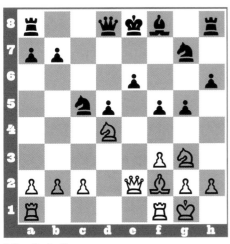

After 3. Qe2

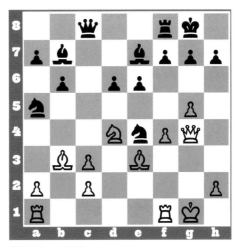

After 3. ... Qc8

In the game, Sevian–Kritz, Dallas, 2015, Black cracked under the pressure: **3. ... f4?** (3. ... Kf7 was necessary), allowing the strong decoy **4. Nh5!**. Black resigned only five moves later.

Black will play ... Nxb3 and will be left with the more active pieces and powerful pawns in the center that restrict White. (4. f5 is answered by 4. ... e5.) The game is Padevsky–Botvinnik, Alekhine Memorial, 1956. Black won in ten more moves.

66 Thus it is that in war the victorious strategist only seeks battle after the victory has been won, whereas he who is destined to defeat first fights and afterwards looks for victory. 99

Chapter 7

The endgame

A chess endgame, or ending, is the final phase of a game that hasn't ended earlier with some sudden catastrophe for one side. The forces are greatly reduced, and there are only a few chessmen left on the board, still looking for a way to win.

66 And if we are able thus to attack an inferior force with a superior one, our opponents will be in dire straits. 99

When material is lopsided, when you're way ahead in an endgame, your opponent won't necessarily give up. These one-sided endgames are like the mop-up after a won military battle.

One side has a big advantage—basic checkmates

In chess, if you don't know how to checkmate, you don't know how to win. On the battlefield, it would be like letting the opposing king escape to reorganize and continue the war against you.

Let's say you've played a long, difficult game and you've out-generaled your opponent so markedly that you're two rooks or a queen ahead—a huge advantage. Wouldn't it be embarrassing not to be able to finish the game off? Your authors have seen countless games where, unfortunately, players did not know how. So let's make sure right now that you have this knowledge. Don't memorize the moves. Remember the ideas behind the moves.

Checkmate with queen and rook

If you're this far ahead, the method is easy. At the same time, it teaches you some basics about all checkmates.

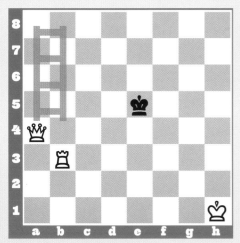

The ladder checkmate

White is so far ahead that the king is not needed for this checkmate, and Black's king can be pushed to the edge of the board quickly. Note how the "queen-and-rook mating machine" rolls forward, pushing the enemy king to the edge row by row, checking on one row and fencing in the row just left behind. **1. Rb5+ Kd6 2. Qa6+ Kc7**. It doesn't matter whether His Highness moves toward the "mating machine" or away from it. The rook is protected by the queen, so the black king can't capture it.

3. Rb7+. The pattern is often called the ladder mate because the movement of White's pieces suggests climbing up a ladder rung by rung. **3. ... Kd8**. Now that the king is at the edge of the board, he has nowhere left to run. **4. Qa8#.**

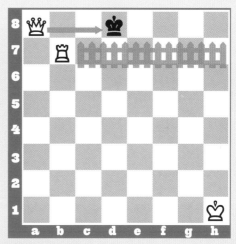

After 4. Qa8#

Checkmate with two rooks

This is the next easiest mating pattern after the checkmate with the queen and rook on the previous page—once again you'll see the ladder pattern, but there's just one twist. Some experts like to call this pattern the "lawnmower mate," because of the way the rooks mow down the rows.

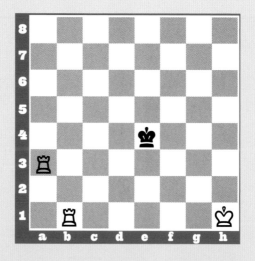

Almost the same as the queen and rook mate on page 113.

Checkmate with the queen

If you're a queen up, checkmating the lone king is still easy. But you have to use your king and know a method (there's more than one). Here's the very first idea you should learn. Look at the position below. Using what you already know, what is White's very best move?

White to move. Cut off the king!

1. Qd7!. Of course, White cuts off the king. It's already on the edge of the board, where it must be to be checkmated. So keep it there! Now Black's king has only three squares to shuffle around on as he waits for the opposing monarch to march up to assist with the *coup de grâce*.
1. ... Kh8. Black would pray for the blunder 2. Qf7?, which would immediately stalemate Black, making a draw! Instead, White calmly brings up the king. **2. Kf2 Kg8 3. Kg3 Kf8 4. Kg4 Kg8 5. Kg5 Kf8 6. Kg6 Kg8 7. Qg7#.**

The "queen sandwich"—a typical mating pattern with king and queen against king.

The attacker does not have to use the king. We're going to show you the easiest mate, not necessarily the fastest, which in this position would make use of the king. (Work this out on your own after you've learned the basics.) **1. Rb4+ Kd5 2. Ra5+ Kc6**. See the difference? Black's king is threatening to capture the rook. So White moves it as far away as possible. **3. Rh5 Kd6 4. Rb6+ Kc7 5. Rg6**. Just like the other rook, this one simply slides out of reach. After all, the rooks can check from afar, but the king has to be on an adjacent square to threaten a rook. **5. ... Kd7 6. Rh7+ Kd8 7. Rg8#**.

What if the enemy king is not already on the edge of the board? Then we need to force it to the edge. A smart defender will stay in the center and then away from the edge as long as possible, because there is no way to be mated there. But if you know the method, you can bully the king to an outer row.

There are several methods. (That makes sense because the queen is so powerful.) But let's learn how to corral the opposing king using only the queen, and then bring up the friendly king, as in the last example. The sequence is called the Knight's Move Method, even though there's no knight on the board. Can you see why?

1. Qf5 Kc6 2. Qe5 Kb7 3. Qd6 Ka7 4. Qc6 Kb8 5. Qd7 Ka8. Did you notice how the easiest way to keep driving the king back was to find a restrictive move with your queen that landed on a knight's move pattern away from the black king? Now, as in the last example, White must avoid 6. Qc7?, stalemating.

6. Kc2 Kb8 7. Kc3 Ka8 8. Kc4 Kb8 9. Kc5 Ka8 10. Kb6 Kb8 11. Qe8#. We could use the "queen sandwich" again, but we wanted to show you a different mating pattern.

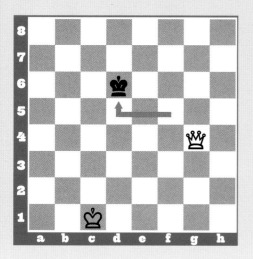

White to move and use the Knight's Move Method.

Checkmate! The black king is fenced in by the white king and placed in check by the white queen.

Checkmate with one rook

One rook and a king are the minimum requirement to force a checkmate against a lone king. A lone knight and king can't checkmate a king; neither can a bishop and king. Learning the king and rook checkmate is a bit more of a challenge than the ones we've seen so far, but it's an absolute must if you want to be any good at chess. And once you get the idea, it's routine.

Let's look first at the end of the mop-up—some typical king-and-rook mating patterns.

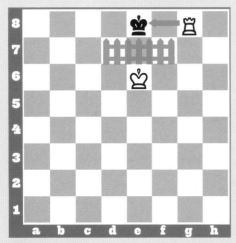
Triangle mate

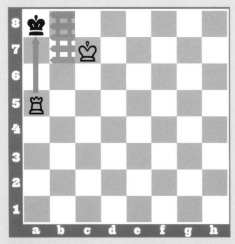
Corner mate

You can see that the defending king needs once again to be forced to the edge of the board. To do this, and to execute the final checkmate, the attacking king and rook need to work as a team. Let's see how they force the king to the edge.

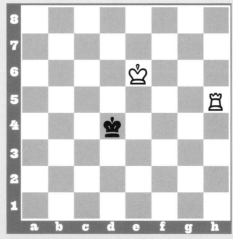
White to move: Build a cage.

1. Re5. The rook builds a box-shaped cage to contain the enemy king. White will use both pieces to make this box smaller and smaller.
1. ... Kd3 2. Kd5 Kc3 3. Re3+ Kb4 4. Rd3 Kb5 5. Rb3+ Ka4. Now that Black's king is on the edge, White needs to set up a mating pattern.
6. Kc4 Ka5 7. Kc5 Ka4 8. Rh3! This waiting move is a key technique. The rook moves away, getting on the other side of its king, while leaving Black only one move. **8. ... Ka5 9. Ra3#**.

If, back on move 7, Black had chosen to run the other way, the technique, and the result, would be the same: 7. ... Ka6 8. Rb4 Ka5 9. Rh4 Ka6 10. Rh7 Ka5 11. Ra7#.

Here's another technique that can come in handy in some situations— what we call the bounce-back trick.

The bounce-back trick

You know that if Black decides on 1. ... Kd8, White immediately checkmates with 2. Rb8#. So, Black runs the other way. **1. ... Kf8 2. Ke6 Kg8 3. Kf6 Kh8 4. Kg6.** Now Black has no choice but to rebound off the other edge of the board into a mating position. **4. ... Kg8 5. Rb8#.**

Tips Checkmate

What to remember when learning how to checkmate with king and rook:

- Use the rook to make a smaller and smaller "box" of squares available to the enemy king.
- Support your rook with your king.
- Force the opposing king to one of the four edges of the board and keep him there— don't let him escape!
- Use the waiting move and bounce-back ideas to set up the checkmate.

Puzzle Rook and king mating

As one more bit of practice with this vital piece of chess knowledge, take the quiz below. Keep in mind that challenges such as mate in three mean implicitly that the defending side makes the best defensive moves.

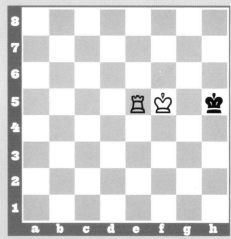

White to move. Find all the moves that mate in three.

Answer

No king moves for White work. But every initial rook move will do! So there are 11 such moves. Make sure to play them all out—you'll cement what you've learned about rook mates. Here are some sample lines. 1.Rd5 Kh4 2.Ra5 Kh5 3.Rh3# or 1. Re1 Kh6 2. Re7 Kh5 3. Rh7#.

Checkmate with two bishops

Checkmate with two bishops is routine, even though it takes a while. It occurs much less frequently than the king and rook checkmate. Here's the method. White can quickly set up a position, with the bishops together, that creates a triangular "fence" (instead of the rectangular cage the rook creates) to restrict the enemy king.

1. Kc4 Kd6 2. Bd5 Ke7 3. Kc5 Kd7 4. Bf6 Ke8 5. Kd6 Kf8 6. Be6 Ke8 7. Ke5. Black can only shuffle back and forth while White maneuvers the king into position to finish the job.

7. ... Kf8 8. Kf5 Ke8 9. Kg6 Kf8 10. Bd7. White forces Black's king into the corner. 10. ... Kg8 11. Be5 Kf8 12. Bd6+ Kg8 13. Be6+ Kh8 14. Be5#.

A two-bishop "fence"

Two-bishop checkmate

When you have to call it a draw

A lone king and bishop can't checkmate on an otherwise bare board, even if the other side makes the worst moves—neither can a lone king and knight. If you're left only with these, the game is automatically drawn. It's called insufficient mating material. Also, two knights and a king cannot *force* mate. But if the defender blunders stupidly, the knights can mate.

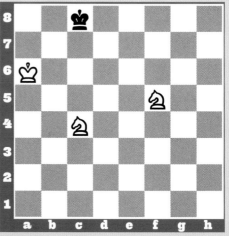

Black self-mates

Checkmate with bishop and knight

Even though two minor pieces are normally stronger than a lone rook, this is the most difficult of the possible mates. Now is a good moment to explain one of the often misunderstood rules of tournament chess: If no captures or pawn moves have been made within the last 50 moves, either player can claim a draw. (But to prove such a claim, the player has to have kept score of each move of the whole game—most likely with the algebraic notation you're reading in this book.) The king, knight, and bishop checkmate can take up to 33 moves if the defending king is in the center of the board, even with perfect play. Just one seriously mistaken move can put the attacker over the limit. So you can see why this rule is important. You have to checkmate within the 50-move limit or concede a draw.

Frankly, there are more practical things for you to learn until you're a high-ranking player, but for the sake of completeness, we'll give you some of the ideas involved. The king must be driven to the edge of the board and to a corner square the same color as the attacker's remaining bishop. Here's an example of the final position.

The final position of a knight and bishop checkmate.

1. Nd4 Kb8 2. Nc6+ Ka8?? Of course Black should not voluntarily move into the corner. If the king stays away from any corner, it can never be checkmated and the game would be drawn. **3. Nb6#.**

A position that should never happen!

> **66** **The control of a large force is the same principle as the control of a few men: it is merely a question of dividing up their numbers. 99**

We chose this quote to admit that everything in war and chess is not the same—and to make the very important point that principles are different in the endgame of chess. It requires an understanding of this disparity to make the transition from the middlegame to a winning endgame.

Three endgame principles

This time we have to disagree with the legendary Sun Tzu, at least as far as chess armies are concerned. In fact, chess endgames have a very different set of guiding principles than the other two stages of a chess game.

When the reduced material of an endgame is pretty even, three of the endgame's most important special principles are:

- The play focuses on promoting a pawn.
- Sometimes it's better not to have to move.
- The king becomes a fighting piece—get it into the battle. (On page 116 you saw how activating the king is necessary even when a player is ahead a whole rook.)

These three ideas don't generally apply to the other two stages of a chess game. In fact, the third principle would be suicide if followed in a stage other than the endgame.

Studying the endgame will result in your chalking up many victories that otherwise would have evaded you. In addition, you'll draw many games you would have lost without this special knowledge. Even masters improve their performance by continually studying the endgame.

Let's take a look at these three principles in action.

Rule of the square

Our first special principle of the endgame is that play often revolves around promoting a pawn. So it would be useful to have a quick way to calculate whether an opposing king can stop an unassisted pawn running for its promotion square. Veteran chess players have such a tool, called the *rule of the square*.

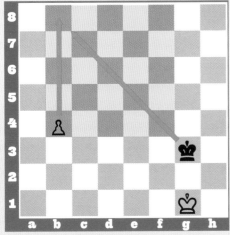

The rule of the square

Counting square by square in your head ("If the pawn moves there, the king moves there") is slow and prone to error. Instead, mentally draw a square box with each side the length of the pawn's projected journey to its queening square. Include the square the pawn is on and the queening square. If the opposing king, on its move, can enter the box, it can catch the pawn. Using this tool, you can see in the diagram above that Black has only one good move, 1. ... Kf4!, after which the king catches the pawn just in time. Try it on your board.

Kings in opposition

Our second special rule of the endgame states that sometimes it's better not to have to move. Look at this seemingly simple position, with White to move. What can we say about it?

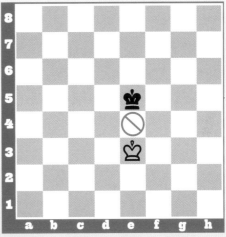

White to move. Black has the opposition.

Of course, if there are only two kings left on the board, the game is a hopeless draw. However, to understand the ideas to come, you must first understand that even just by His Royal Self, a king can sometimes shoulder his counterpart, similarly to a football lineman rushing past the opposition to get to any part of the field.

The above diagram illustrates a fundamental weapon of the endgame. Note that there is one square between the two monarchs. (That's as close as kings can ever come to one another, because moving closer would be moving into check—illegal of course.) One king will have to move back or to the side, giving way. (Recall we wrote that in an endgame, sometimes it's better not to have to move.) This fact is so important in chess endgames that we have a special name for the situation: *the opposition*. Since White has to move, we say Black has the opposition. (If, in this same position, it were Black's move, then White would have the opposition.)

The king with the opposition can move to any part of the board. Alternatively, it can block its rival from any part of the board. Let's pretend that White's first rank is the goal line in a game of American football. Black tries to score. Of course White tries to stop this: **1. Kd3 Kf4**. Black outflanks White. **2. Ke2 Ke4**. Taking the opposition again. **3. Kf2 Kd3 4. Ke1 Ke3**. Grabbing the opposition yet again. **5. Kf1 Kd2 6. Kf2 Kd1**. Touchdown. No matter which squares White had chosen to fall back to, Black could have followed the same procedure to force the king through to the first rank: flanking, gaining the opposition, flanking, and repeat.

Now look at this position.

Here the black king seems quite distant from his goal. But the kings still face each other on the same file. Count the squares between the kings—three. It's an odd number, so whoever does not have to move still has the opposition. When there is more than one square between kings, we can call it the *distant opposition*. Work this out on your own board using the same techniques you just learned, and you'll prove to yourself that Black can again score the touchdown.

Activate your king

Both opposition and the rule of the square demonstrate our third special rule of the endgame: activate your king.

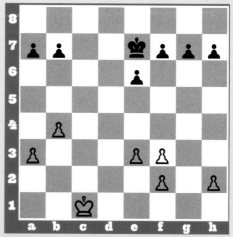

Erich Cohn v. Akiba Rubinstein, St. Petersburg 1909. After 25. Kxc1

Although material is equal, White has a weak, isolated pawn on h2. Here Polish Grandmaster Akiba Rubinstein immediately shows the value in using the king for a fighting piece when there is insufficient enemy material on the board to harass His Majesty.

Earlier Cohn traded rooks, and that was a fatal mistake. Rooks are almost always a drawing factor in contrast with pure pawn endgames. Instead, he left himself with a bare-bones and inferior pawn ending. He may have wanted to avoid any rook-and-pawn ending with Rubinstein, who was renowned for his mastery of such endgames. (After one such miraculous win, a tongue-in-cheek annotator suggested that in previous times, Rubinstein would have been burned as a witch.)
25. ... Kf6 26. Kd2 Kg5 27. Ke2 Kh4 28. Kf1 Kh3. Straightforward and logical play.

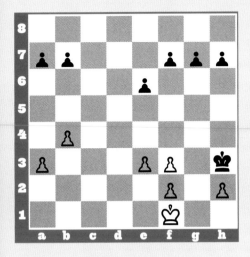

Whether White captures or pushes his f-pawn, Black will use his better-positioned king to win. If 39. fxg3, for example, then 39. ... Kxg3, and Black will win the pawn on e4, queen a pawn and use its awesome powers to win the game easily. One interesting variation you may enjoy: **39. f4 exf4 40. e5 g2 41. e6 Kg3 42. e7 f3 43. e8=Q f2#**. White queens first, but Black mates with his pawns!

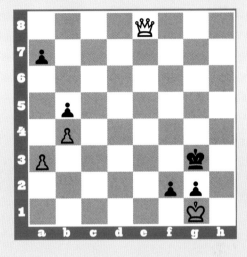

29. Kg1 (White's king reaches his pawn to guard it just in time. But now he's tethered to it.) **29. ... e5 30. Kh1 b5** (Notice how Rubinstein positions his b-pawn to restrain both of White's queenside pawns.) **31. Kg1 f5** (Whatever White tries, the outcome is the same. Black will advance and exchange his own kingside pawns until he can capture the last of White's kingside pawns, leaving him a crucial pawn up.) **32. Kh1 g5 33. Kg1 h5 34. Kh1 g4 35. e4 fxe4 36. fxe4 h4 37. Kg1 g3 38. hxg3 hxg3 White resigns.**

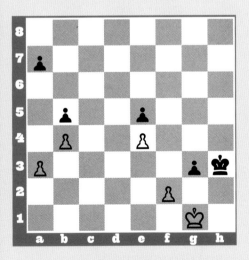

66 To see victory only when it is within the ken of the common herd is not the acme of excellence. 99

The results of a battle between near equals can come down to small things—the precise timing of a reserve cavalry charge, or the advantage of a single pawn. After a long, hard struggle on the chessboard, it's frustrating and even embarrassing, not to know how to drive home such an advantage, or understand how to salvage the draw.

Basic endgames

It's not an exaggeration to tell you that what we will look at next is a building block for nearly all endgames: endings in which one side has an extra pawn—a potential queen—that can be assisted by its king. Such endgames often occur in games between evenly matched players. Let's look at the bare bones of such an ending, when there is a lone king against a king and pawn. These endgames are the basis for much more complicated positions, so knowing these endings is eminently practical.

Three seems to be a magic number in the chess endgame. There are, again, three principles that will help you find the right plans in such situations.

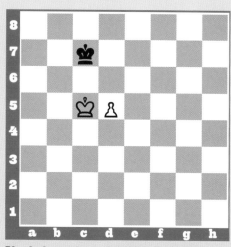

Black draws by not letting the white king in front of the pawn.

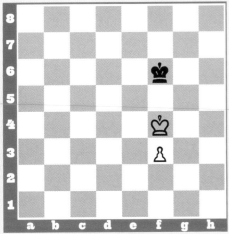

Black to move loses. White to move draws.

If the strong king can get in front of his pawn

- If the king of the stronger side can get in front of the pawn, that will be enough to win—unless the defender can gain the opposition.

If Black is to move in the position above, the king must give way. White will then use the standard method of flanking and gaining the opposition

If the strong king can't get in front of his pawn

- If the king of the stronger side can't get in front of his pawn, the game is probably a draw with best play.

Regardless of whose move it is, White cannot force a win in the diagram. If it's Black's move, the only saving move is **1. ... Kd7!**, but it's easy to see this if you know the principle—*get in front of the pawn so that your opponent can't.* Since White can't make progress with the king, the alternative is to try to push the pawn. The method Black then uses to draw is fundamental: **2. d6 Kd8!** (not 2. ... Kc8 3. Kc6 Kd8 4. d7

to secure access to the queening square: **1. ... Ke6 2. Kg5 Kf7 3. Kf5 Ke7 4. Kg6 Kf8 5. Kf6 Ke8 6. Kg7**. White's king has gained control of the queening square. The only thing Black can do is dodge to the side and try to intercept the pawn, but that attempt is futile. **6. ... Kd7**. If 6. Ke7, then White wins by 7. f4 Ke6 8. Kg6 Ke7 9. f5 Kf8 10. Kf6!, seizing the opposition. Whichever way Black's king moves, White's king outflanks it and the pawn marches ahead to f8. **7. Kf7 Kd6 8. f4 Kd7 9. f5 Kd6 10. f6 Kd7 11. Kg7 Ke8 12. f7+ Ke7 13. f8=Q+**. And you know what will happen once White has a queen.

Now let's go back to the diagram above to see what happens if it's White's move—in other words, if Black has the opposition. It's a bit of a dance, really, as Black again and again uses the opposition to frustrate White's intentions.

1. Ke4 Ke6 2. f4 Kf6 3. f5 Kf7 4. Ke5 Ke7 5. f6+ Kf7 6. Kf5. Compare this position to the diagram on page 124 and you won't be surprised by the outcome. **6. ... Kf8 7. Kg6 Kg8 8. f7+ Kf8 9. Kf6 stalemate.**

Ke7 5. Kc7 when White queens the pawn) **3. Kc6 Kc8 4. d7+ Kd8**. Here there are no winning choices. White can abandon the pawn and draw immediately through insufficient winning material, or play Kd6 and draw immediately with stalemate.

If it's White's move in the position on page 124, knowing the defensive technique again saves the game for Black. **1. d6+ Kd7 2. Kd5**. Forced, or Black will simply capture the pawn, which would end the game immediately in a draw. **2. ... Kd8!**. Black again finds the only move to hold the draw because this ensures that Black will gain the opposition whether White tries 3. Ke6 or 3. Kc6; for example: 3. Ke6 Ke8 4. d7+ Kd8. Now either White abandons the pawn or plays **3. Kd6 stalemate.**

If the strong king can reach the sixth rank

- If the king of the stronger side can reach the sixth rank directly or diagonally ahead of the pawn, this wins, regardless of who has the opposition.

White wins no matter who is to move.

The drawing power of rook pawns

The term "rook pawns," signifying the the pawns that start the game in front of rooks, is a common expression to identify the a- and h-pawns. Rook pawns are odd ducks in the king and pawn endings. Because the action is on the edge of the board, as the enemy pawn and king advance toward the queening square, the threats of stalemate are constant. Here's a simple illustration.

As you've learned, if we moved the pieces just one square to the left (toward the queenside), White would win easily. But here Black is stalemated. A categorical rule in king-and-pawn endgames is that when the extra pawn is a rook pawn, the defender can draw whenever the king can get in front of the pawn. Indeed, sometimes even when the side with the extra pawn can get the king ahead of the pawn, the game can still be drawn!

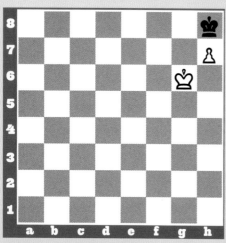

Black to move: stalemate.

Draw no matter who is to move.

After all you've learned, it might seem on first glance that this position would hinge on the opposition. But because Black is backed up against the edge of the board and has limited options, the game is lost no matter who is to move. Of course, if it's Black's move, the win is easy: **1. ... Kd8** (1. ... Kf8 2. Kd7) **2. Kf7**, and the pawn waltzes in.

If it's White's move, both 1. Kd6 and 1. Kf6 win: **1. Kd6 Kd8 2. e6 Ke8 3. e7**. Here there's no stalemate, and Black is squeezed off the queening square. **3. ... Kf7 4. Kd7**, and White promotes on the next move.

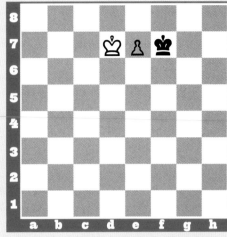

After 4. Kd7: White will queen the pawn.

At first glance, White seems to be in the driver's seat. But, regardless of who's on move, the game is an easy draw for Black. If it's Black's move, **1. ... Kf5!** (of course, now if White advances the king with 2. Kh6, the simple 2. ... Kg4 wins the pawn) **2. h4 Kf6 3. Kh6 Kf7 4. Kh7 Kf8 5. h5** (if 5. Kg6, Black gets into the corner with 5. Kg8 and can never be forced out, only stalemated) **5. ... Kf7 6. h6 Kf8 7. Kh8 Kf7 8. h7 Kf8** stalemate.

White is stalemated.

Distant passed pawns

So an extra rook pawn—in these reduced endings—often can only result in a draw, if the defending king is in front of the pawn or can stymie progress from the flank. But let's look at a position with a few more pawns on the board. You'll see that what we call a *distant passed pawn* can be quite deadly as a decoy. A passed pawn is simply a pawn that can advance without being blocked or captured by another pawn. In the next diagram, White's a-pawn is passed. And it is also distant from the rest of the action.

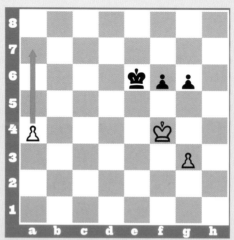

Here the distant passed pawn wins by decoying Black's king.

Here material is equal. Black's pawns are united, while White's are isolated. That could be to White's disadvantage in the middlegame. But, as we've said, the endgame has its own principles.

1. a5! Forcing Black to move the king inside the square of the pawn to stop it from queening. **1. ... Kd6 2. a6 Kc6 3. a7 Kb7 4. Ke4 Kxa7.** White has pushed the a-pawn until it was captured. But now the black king has been pulled away from the defense of its own pawns. **5. Kd5 Kb7 6. Ke6 Kc7 7. Kxf6 Kd7 8. Kxg6 Ke7 9. Kg7 Ke6.** White makes it easy by *shouldering* the enemy king away from the queening square. You know how this story ends.

Make a passed pawn

Since passed pawns are the torpedoes of the endgame, make them when you can.

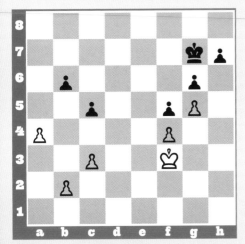

White to move and win.

Again, material is even. But with 1. b4!, White makes a distant passed pawn, which will decoy Black's king, and wins. Work this out on your own board.

   Hint: Consider that Black's king is outside the square of White's a-pawn.

Pawn breakthrough

Remember that you can sacrifice a lot of material to queen a pawn and still come out way ahead. With that in mind, what's the best move in this position?

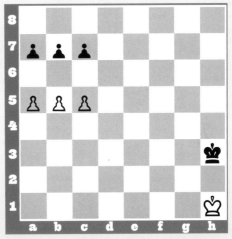

White to move. What's your evaluation?

You might think Black would have the upper hand because the king can move back to attack the white pawns. But because White's pawns are so far advanced, a breakthrough sacrifice is possible. **1. b6! axb6 2. c6!.** If 2. … bxa6, then 3. a6. If 3. … bxa5, then 3. cxb7. And if back on the first move, Black had tried 1. … cxb6, 2. a6! will come to the same end. However Black reacts, White will queen a pawn and mop up long before Black's pawns can threaten to queen.

   You've learned some important basics of the pawn endings—the skeleton of all chess endgames.

> **66** Hence, though an obstinate fight may be made by a small force, in the end it must be captured by the larger force. **99**

Endgames are usually won by the side with the most material—or *potential material*! A rose may be a rose, but a pawn about to queen is often more than a pawn. The interplay between pieces and aspiring pawns makes up a wonderful world of chess technique.

Pieces and pawns in the endgame

The imbalance that exists between a pawn, as a potential queen, and the enemy pieces is one of the bewitching dimensions of chess. At the beginning of a game, we assign the lowly pawn a numerical value of one and the queen nine. So, in an endgame, how do you value a pawn on the march to promote itself to a queen? There are some guidelines that can help us. But you'll have to analyze the specifics of your own games.

Minor piece versus a single pawn

Some games come down to a minor piece versus a pawn. You already know that a minor piece can't checkmate even with the help of its king, so with rare exceptions in such endings, the player with the piece should capture the lone pawn at the first opportunity, ending the game. In the diagram below, White should capture on b1 the moment the pawn is promoted on that square.

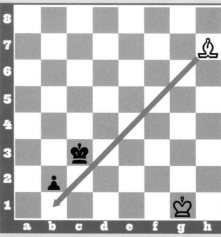

White will capture the pawn and secure a draw.

Queen versus pawn

When the piece is a major piece (a queen or a rook), the side with the single pawn would normally love to draw, since a major piece can give checkmate with the help of the king. A queen versus a pawn will almost always win by arranging to capture the pawn and then forcing checkmate. But there are exceptions when the side with the pawn has advanced a rook or bishop pawn all the way to the next-to-last rank.

In the top diagram at left, after **1. ... Ka1!**, White must move off the b-file or give stalemate. Black then plays **2. ... Kb1**, threatening to promote. White can't make progress. In the second diagram, if White captures the pawn, the game ends immediately in stalemate. Again, no headway can be made with other moves. Pawns about to queen on files other than the rook and bishop files can't arrange the same stalemate trick. Stalemate themes are fascinating—and can be frustrating when you're trying to bring home your advantage.

If the stronger side's king is closer to the queening square, a win is possible because the king supports checkmating threats.

Black plays 1. ... Ka1! and draws.

With the white king closer, Black loses.

1. ... Ka1 (1. ... Kc1 loses even more quickly: 2. Qb4 Kd1 3. Qd2#) **2. Qa3+ Kb1 3. Qb4+ Kc1 4. Qb5 Kd1 5. Qf1#.**

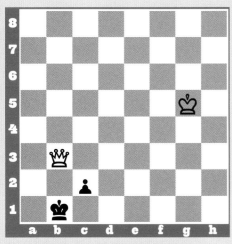

Black plays 1. ... Ka1! and draws.

Rook versus pawn

The less powerful major piece, the rook, normally wins against a lone pawn and king. The stronger side will always win when the king is in front of the enemy pawn. But when the stronger side's king is far from the action, there are exceptions. In the diagram below, White wins because Black's king can be cut off from the 5th rank.

White wins with 1. Rg5!.

Black can't reach the pawn to defend it. If it stands still, White simply brings the king up the board to capture it. And if the pawn moves forward, the rook wins it: **1. ... b3 2. Rb5.**

But if it's Black's move, **1. ... Kc4** draws, because the king now protects its prize possession and nurses it forward until the white rook must exchange itself for the potential queen. But remember, in positions where the white king can get in front of such a pawn, White wins easily.

Multiple pawns versus a piece

When one side has more than one pawn against a piece, chess life gets more complicated, but some principles remain the same. King position is again crucial. Let's look at an interesting example of two pawns versus a rook when the kings are both out of play.

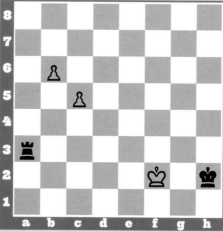

Whichever side moves first wins.

First of all, we'll point out that if Black's king were in front of the enemy pawns, say on b7, Black would win easily by attacking the pawns with the rook and capturing them. On the other hand, if White's king were ahead of the pawns, for example on c7, at least one of the pawns would promote and White would win.

But back to the diagram, where the kings aren't a factor: If it's White to move, either **1. c6** or **1. b7** wins, since the rook can't stop both pawns. If it's Black's move, **1. ... Rb3!** will win both pawns. (If White moves the king, then Black plays **2. ... Rb5!** and the pawns fall). Play this out on your board.

This next position shows you some of the basic ideas when a bishop defends against multiple pawns.

The bishop can even draw against three pawns when conditions are right.

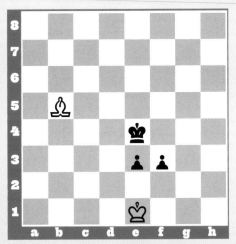

White draws, whoever moves first.

White draws, whoever moves first.

We've already seen that, against one pawn, the bishop simply captures it at the first opportunity for a draw. But here Black has two potential queens. Nevertheless, with good play, White draws.

    1. ... e2 would quickly permit White to dissolve any threat of the enemy's queening: **2. Bxe2 fxe2 3. Kxe2**. If instead **1. ... Kf4**, trying to help with the king, White can play **2. Kf1 Kg3 3. Ke1 Kg2 4. Bc6**, and Black can't make progress. Finally, if **1. ... f2+,** White plays **2. Kf1** and then shuttles the bishop back and forth along the a6–f1 diagonal, forming an unbreakable blockade.

Some sample lines: **1. ... e4 2. Kf2 Ke5 3. Kg3 f4+** (if 3. ... Kd4 4. Bd7 f4+ 5. Kf2 e3+ 6. Ke2 Ke5 7. Kf3, and Black's progress is stymied) **4. Kg4 Kd4 5. Kxg5 f3 6. Kf4 f2 7. Kg3 e3 8. Kf3**, when Black is again unable to force either promotion.

    But if you moved Black's whole army one square forward, Black would win pretty easily. Analyze that position on your own.

Here's another illustration that endgame principles can be very different from those of the opening and middlegame. We've learned that in the first two of the game's three stages, isolated pawns—pawns that have no friendly pawns to protect them—are often a weakness. But in the endgame, isolated pawns can be powerful.

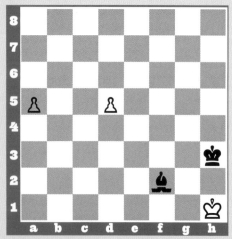

Widely separated pawns. White wins, whoever moves.

Even with the move, Black can't stop the pawns; for example, **1. ... Bc5 2. a6 Kg4 3. d6 Bxd6 4. a7**, and the monochromatic bishop is helpless to prevent the pawn promotion.

However, move the pawn on a5 to b5, and Black can stop the pawns easily; for example, **1. ... Bc5 2. d6 Bxd6 3. Kg1** (3. b6 Be5 4. b7 Bd6 5. b8=Q Bxb8) **3. ... Bc5+**, when Black's bishop will snap off the pawn whenever it steps to the next square. If it never does, of course, the game is also drawn.

Knight and pawn

In the position below, White must queen the pawn in order to win. But after 1. a7?, even though the pawn is protected, the black king simply shuffles between b7 and a8 and can't be forced out of the corner. Then if White's king approaches too closely, it's stalemate.

White to move and win.

1. Nb4! is the right way, defending the pawn from behind on the sixth rank. Now White can advance the king without stalemating, and, once the pawn is supported by the king, the knight can force the black king out of the corner: **1. Nb4 Kb8 2. Kc2 Ka8 3. Kc3 Kb8 4. Kc4 Ka8 5. Kc5 Ka7 6. Kc6 Kb8 7. Kb6 Ka8 8. Nd5 Kb8 9. Nc7.** White promotes and then checkmates with the new queen.

Now let's take a look at a famous position composed by Alexey Troitsky in 1906. (Chess players call this kind of puzzle an *endgame study*). As you know, a knight and king can't checkmate a lone king. But if that king has one rook pawn left in its army, about to reach the queening square, ironically a surprising checkmate can occur.

White to move and force checkmate!

1. Kf3! Kh1 2.Kf2 Kh2 3.Nc3 (The goal is the f1-square.) **3. ... Kh1 4. Ne4 Kh2 5.Nd2 Kh1 6. Nf1 h2 7. Ng3#.** The black king is trapped by its own pawn.

1. Kf2? instead would be a big mistake. After 1. ... Kh1 2. Ng3+ Kh2 3. Ne4 Kh1, White would have blown the chance to checkmate because a knight cannot "lose" a tempo to pass the move, as a bishop can. That's too bad for White in this last position, because if it were Black's move, it would be checkmate after 4. ... Kh2 5. Nd2 Kh1 6. Nf1 h2 7. Ng3#.

When it comes to multiple pieces and pawns, the specifics of the position determine best play, but the basic principles will help you find the right plan. In general, the more material on the board, the more chance the player with even a small advantage has of winning.

When you play over master games, pay particular attention to their handling of the endgame. As you gain experience in your own games, you'll learn what works and what doesn't. At the end of this book, we recommend some books that are dedicated to endgame play and so have space to teach you a lot more about this critical part of chess.

Tips Endgame

As long as you remain with enough material to mate, being a piece up should win. But some kinds of endgames are hard to win even when you are a pawn or two ahead. The most "drawish" of such endgames are called "opposite-color bishops" endings. That term means the opponents each have one bishop, but each bishop travels on different color squares. The next-hardest to win are endings where both sides have a rook or two. Always keep these points in mind in the endgame.

- Visualize a plan and make moves based on that plan.
- Activate your king!
- Try to promote a pawn so that you have enough material to win by checkmating your opponent.
- If you have a passed pawn, push it! (Of course, don't just push it to lose it.)
- If you don't have a passed pawn, create one if you can.
- Put your king in front of a passed pawn, and your rook, if you have one, behind it (whether the pawn is yours or your opponent's).
- If you're behind in material, trade pawns, not pieces.
- If you're ahead in material, trade pieces, not pawns.

66 **There are not more than five primary colors, yet in combination they produce more hues than can ever be seen.** 99

Chapter 8

Model campaigns

In getting this far, you've reviewed the backbone of chess mastery. As a result, we would guess that you're already good enough to beat most of the opponents you'll cross pawns with in your travels. To continue to improve, however—to get really good at chess—you should do two things. You should practice, by playing lots of games, and you should play over master games. You've already seen some famous ones as illustrations of the ideas in the previous chapters.

The half-dozen famous games in this section are among the most brilliant and instructive ever contested. Play through each on your board a number of times. The first time you play through a game, go through the main line—the moves in bold type—fairly quickly, getting the gist of the game. (As always, use the diagrams to check that you have the correct positions on your own board.) Don't worry about side-variations in the notes. Then go back to move 1 and give the game a closer look, only then playing over sidelines.

Come back to all of these games often, since they merit your attention again and again. As you continue to study them, you'll see that the great masters use the very same tools you've learned.

66 The prime object of attacking with fire is to throw the enemy into confusion. If this effect is not produced, it means that the enemy is ready to receive us. Hence the necessity for caution. 99

Evergreen game

White attacks with the chess equivalent of fire in the following game—and his enemy is indeed thrown into confusion.

Modern military leaders still study the battle plans of Alexander the Great and Napoleon. In the same way, some chess games will be studied as long as there are chess players. But unlike military leaders of old, earlier chess players had the very same weaponry as their modern descendants.

This game is one of Adolf Anderssen's most celebrated masterpieces. He was considered the strongest chess player in the world before the American Paul Morphy came along to defeat him, along with every other leading master who would take up the challenge. Anderssen's opponent, Jean Dufresne, was a strong master, a student of Anderssen's and a very popular writer on chess.

In their era, full-blooded attack, like fearless infantry charges on the battlefield, was the most admired approach. You'll see that in this wonderful melée, the adversaries use their armies to go all-out after the opposing king. Notice also that the loser is the player who never gets castled!

ADOLF ANDERSSEN (PRUSSIA) V **JEAN DUFRESNE** (GERMANY)
NEW ORLEANS, 1852

1. e4 e5 2. Nf3 Nc6 3. Bc4 Bc5

Classical development in the form of the Giuoco Piano—occupy the center and develop minor pieces to bear on the center squares.

4. b4

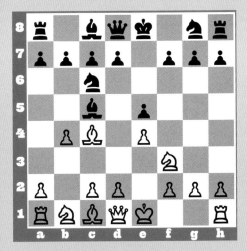

Anderssen plays the Evans Gambit, popular in his era and still dangerous today. He offers a pawn for an enduring initiative.

4. ... Bxb4 5. c3 Ba5 6. d4 exd4 7. 0–0 d3

Taking the pawn on c3 was also reasonable.

8. Qb3

White's queen and bishop create a battery that attacks the f7 square, a weak point since Black hasn't yet castled.

8. ... Qf6 9. e5

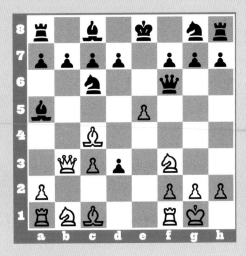

9. ... Qg6

Black can't safely capture the impudent e-pawn. If 9. ... Nxe5 10. Re1 d6 11. Qa4+, with a double attack that snares the bishop.

10. Re1 Nge7 11. Ba3

11. ... b5

Most modern masters would castle. But Dufresne wants to mix things up, opening the b-file for his rook and developing his own kingside attack by developing his light-square bishop to b7. Another reason he likes b5 is that it disrupts the battery aiming at his f7.

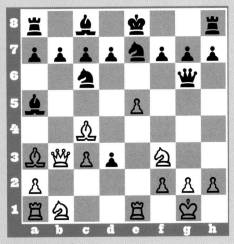

After 11. Ba3

**12. Qxb5 Rb8 13. Qa4 Bb6
14. Nbd2 Bb7**

Discretion would now be the better part of valor. Black should castle. But one of Dufresne's fellow Berliners, the chess master Bernhard Horwitz, was famous for attacking in this way, with bishops on adjacent diagonals. In fact the arrangement is still called "Horwitz bishops." Here we see Horwitz's obvious influence on Dufresne.

15. Ne4 Qf5!?

Black has no easy moves—White's pieces dominate the center.

16. Bxd3

White threatens both 17. Nd6+ and 17. Nf6+, discovering an attack on the black queen.

16. ... Qh5 17. Nf6+

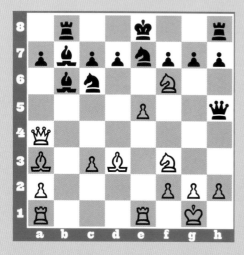

17. ... gxf6

Black must accept the knight sacrifice, since otherwise the queen and king are forked.

18. exf6 Rg8!

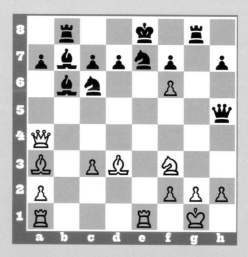

Black's rook jumps onto the g-file. Because he's pinned the g-pawn, Black threatens 19. ... Qxf3. It seems Dufresne's dream of a counter-attack is coming true.

19. Rad1!

This move sets a fiendish trap, anticipating that Black will go for what seems an obvious win.

19. ... Qxf3

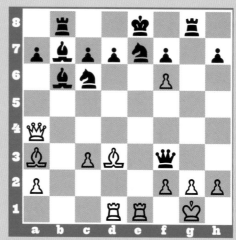

Black wins the white knight and threatens mate in one—but this move loses! Black could have kept the game even with a queen move that doesn't capture the knight: 19. ... Qh3 20. Bf1 Qf5, protecting d7. (You'll soon see why this is important.)

20. Rxe7+!! Nxe7

Black had no defense. If 20. ... Kf8, then the discovered attack 21. Re3+ would win the queen. And here's a beautiful line that Anderssen had to have in mind: 20. ... Kd8 21. Rxd7+ Kc8 22. Rd8+ Nxd8 23. Qd7+ Kxd7 24. Bf5+ Ke8 (if 24. ... Kc6, then 25. Bd7#) 25. Bd7#. Relentless!

21. Qxd7+!!

22. ... Ke8 23. Bd7+ Kf8
24. Bxe7#

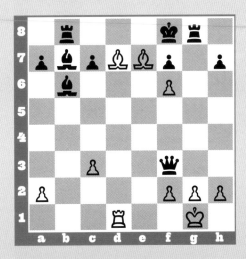

Black threatened mate in one but never had the chance to pull the trigger!

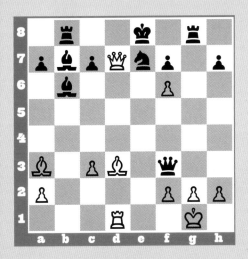

21. ... Kxd7 22. Bf5+
Double check!

66 To mystify, mislead, and surprise the enemy is one of the first principles in war. 99

Marshall's magic

No one could mystify an opponent more than Frank Marshall—and in this game he may have played his most surprising move of all.

One of the most famous games in chess literature, this barn-burner features a legion of imaginative tactics. The legend (most likely an exaggeration) is that after Marshall's 23rd move, the appreciative spectators showered the chessboard with gold coins.

Marshall was US chess champion for 27 years, and one of the strongest players in the world. Levitsky was also a very strong player, in fact, the Russian national champion. These days, he's known only for being on the wrong side of Marshall's flabbergasting 23rd move.

STEPAN LEVITSKY (RUSSIA) V FRANK MARSHALL (USA)
BRESLAU, POLAND, 1912

1. e4 e6 2. d4 d5
The French Defense, as discussed on page 40. At the cost of blocking in his light-square bishop, Black secures his center pawn on d5 and opens up a diagonal for his other bishop.

3. Nc3 c5
Marshall played frisky chess, always looking for a game full of tricks and swindles. As a result, there are "Marshall Gambits" in many opening variations. This is one.

4. Nf3 Nc6 5. exd5 exd5 6. Be2
Pinning the knight with 6. Bb5 was a bit better, but White's move is reasonable development.

6. ... Nf6 7. 0–0 Be7 8. Bg5 0–0 9. dxc5

Saddling Black with an isolated pawn.

9. ... Be6 10. Nd4

This move starts a bad strategy—trading the knight for the bishop on e6, which strengthens Black's center.

10. ... Bxc5 11. Nxe6 fxe6
12. Bg4 Qd6 13. Bh3

Now that the black queen is no longer pinned, White must move his light-square bishop to preserve it.

13. ... Rae8 14. Qd2 Bb4

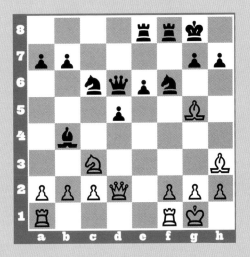

With the threat of d4, winning the pinned knight.

**15. Bxf6 Rxf6 16. Rad1 Qc5
17. Qe2 Bxc3 18. bxc3 Qxc3
19. Rxd5**

White takes advantage of his pin. Now if 19. ... exd5?, 20. Qxe8+.

19. ... Nd4
An in-between move.

20. Qh5

White has to give up the pin on the e-file and so leaves his own rook *en prise*. But he hopes to maintain the balance by counter-attacking Black's

rook on e8. Later analysis showed that 20. Qe5 was best. If 20. Qe4 Rf4 21. Qf4, then Black has 21, ... Ne2+, the Royal Knight Fork!

20. ... Ref8
Black doubles his rooks on the f-file. He threatens 21. ... Rxf2, because 22. Rxf2 allows 22. ... Qe1+ 23. Rf1 Qxf1#.

**21. Re5 Rh6 22. Qg5 Rxh3!
23. Rc5**

23. gxh3 Nf3+ 24. Kg2 Nxg5

23. ... Qg3!! White resigns
Other moves win, but not with the same impertinence! Black plops down his queen where it can be taken by two different pawns or the enemy queen—yet every white move loses.

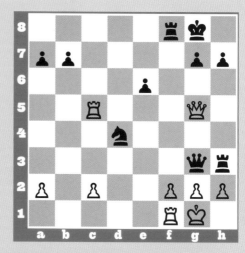

Black threatens 24. ... Qxh2#. Any move by White's rook on f1 loses to 24... Qxh2+ 25.Kf1 Qh1#. If 24.f4 (or 24.f3), then 24. ... Ne2+ 25. Kh1 Qxh2#. If 24. hxg3 Ne2#. If 24. fxg3 Ne2+ 25.Kh1 Rxf1#—a back-rank mate! If 24. hxg3 Ne2 #. And if 24. Qxg3 Ne2+ 25.Kh1 Nxg3+ 26.Kg1 (if 26.fxg3 Rxf1#) Nxf1 27.gxh3 Nd2, and Black will keep his extra piece. Not wanting to see any of this played out against him over the board, Black resigned.

66 Thus the expert in battle moves the enemy, and is not moved by him. 99

In the following game—or was it a composition?—White brilliantly "moves the enemy," offering a queen sacrifice to deflect Black's most powerful piece from the defense of his back rank. Resist as he might, Black is eventually forced to capitulate.

Grandmaster deflection or deception?

Edwin Adams v Carlos Torre is another world-famous game many masters know by heart. Not a tournament contest, it was played as a "skittles," or offhand game. But was it even an actual game? The mystery is tantalizing. Carlos Torre was a famous Mexican champion who played brilliant games in the US and Europe. But in this game, he was the loser—and the winner was his principal financial sponsor. There is no record of E.Z. Adams ever playing another notable game of chess. One theory is that the idea grew out of a practice matchup between the two men and was developed into a dazzling "game" by the modest Torre.

So was the famous series of queen sacrifices Torre's homage to his benefactor, or was it the kind of "lightning in a bottle" that sometimes happens to mediocre representatives of any sport? It's likely to remain, as the great Bobby Fischer was once described, "A mystery wrapped in an enigma." Somehow the riddle makes studying the game (or composition) even more captivating. Whether an actual game or an inspiration that grew out of an offhand game and into a delightful study, there's no more famous deflection.

EDWIN ADAMS (USA) V CARLOS TORRE
(MEXICO)
NEW ORLEANS, 1920

1. e4 e5 2. Nf3 d6
You saw Philidor's Defense in Paul
Morphy's famous opera-box game
on page 65.

3. d4 exd4
Torre decides to give up his center
pawn.

4. Qxd4
4. Nxd4 is also a good choice.

4. ... Nc6 5. Bb5

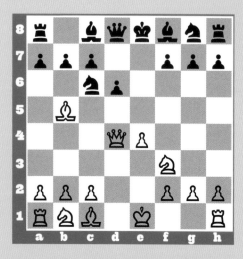

White develops with a pin on the
knight rather than moving the queen
from the center.

**5. ... Bd7 6. Bxc6 Bxc6 7. Nc3
Nf6 8. 0–0 Be7 9. Nd5 Bxd5
10. exd5 0–0 11. Bg5 c6 12. c4
cxd5 13. cxd5 Re8 14. Rfe1 a5
15. Re2 Rc8?**

White has signaled his intent to
double rooks on the e-file. Black
should have played 15. ... h6,
making *luft* to avoid the threats of
back-rank mate.

16. Rae1 Qd7 17. Bxf6 Bxf6

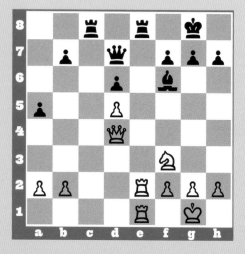

18. Qg4!
Offering a queen sacrifice as a deflection! Not simply the best move, but the only move that forces a win. But why can White put his queen *en prise*?

18. ... Qb5
Here's why: If instead 18. ... Qxg4, White would mate in two with 19. Rxe8+ Rxe8 20. Rxe8#. Black sees that he can't accept the queen sacrifice and moves away from the white queen's suicide attack. But notice that Black's queen must stay tethered to the protection of e8. It's also worth noting that if 18. ... Qd8 19. Qxc8 Rxe2 20. Qxd8+ Bxd8 21. Rxe2, and White is a rook up.

19. Qc4!!
White again offers the queen sacrifice, tempting Black from the protection of e8—this time the queen can be captured with either queen or rook!

19. ... Qd7
If 19. ... Qxc4 20. Rxe8+ Rxe8 21. Rxe8#; if 19. ... Rxc4 20. Rxe8+ Qxe8 21. Rxe8#; and if 19. ... Rxe2 20. Qxc8+ Qe8 21. Qxe8+ Rxe8 22. Rxe8#.

20. Qc7!!

What a delightfully in-your-face deflection! Of course, after either 20. ... Qxc7 or 20. ... Rxc7, White would play 21. Rxe8+ and 22. Rxe8 checkmate!

20. ... Qb5
By now you know the theme: if 20. ... Rxc7 21. Rxe8+ Qxe8 22. Rxe8#; if 20. ... Qxc7 21. Rxe8+ Rxe8 22. Rxe8#; and if 20. ... Rxe2 21. Qxd7 Rxe1+ 22. Nxe1, when White has an overwhelming material advantage.

21. a4!
But not 21. Qxb7?, when Black suddenly turns the tables on White with 21. ... Qxe2 22. Rxe2 Rc1+, checkmating him in two more moves.

21. ... Qxa4 22. Re4!! Qb5
There's still no way out for Black: if 22. ... Rf8 23. Qxc8 Qxe4 24. Qxf8+ Kxf8 25. Rxe4; or if 22. ... h6 23. Qxc8 Rxc8 24.Rxa4.

23. Qxb7! Black resigns.

Now it's truly "an offer you can't refuse"—or in this case, accept. After this last in a series of moves that leaves the white queen *en prise*, Black's queen can no longer find a safe square to support the rook on e8. White will checkmate on the back rank: 23. ... Qxb7 24. Rxe8+ Rxe8 25. Rxe8#.

> **66** Hence, when able to attack, we must seem unable; when using our forces, we must seem inactive; when we are near, we must make the enemy believe we are far away; when far away, we must make him believe we are near. **99**

I'm winning, right?

Bobby Fischer made his chessmen seem unable and far away in this celebrated brilliancy—so much so that even the onlookers thought Fischer's opponent was winning!

Fischer was likely the most famous chess player of all time. His 1972 victory over the Soviet Union's Boris Spassky in Reykjavik, Iceland, for the World Championship at the height of the Cold War captured worldwide attention. Of all the marvelous games that Fischer played, this is our favorite. It was played in the 1964 US Championship, which Fischer won with a score of 11–0, the only perfect score in the event's history.

Grandmaster Robert Byrne played White. Byrne, a university English professor, was also one of the country's elite chess players. He later won both the US Championship and qualified as a world championship candidate. But he became most well-known for writing the chess column for the *New York Times'* for nearly 30 years.

An amusing aspect of this contest is that both Byrne and the grandmaster commentators, in a special room for the public, were convinced to the very end that Fischer was losing.

ROBERT BYRNE (USA) V **ROBERT FISCHER** (USA)
NEW YORK CITY, 1963

1. d4 Nf6 2. c4 g6 3. g3 c6 4. Bg2 d5 5. cxd5
A variation of the King's Indian Defense in which White fianchettoes his light-squared bishop to pressure the queenside.

5. ... cxd5 6. Nc3 Bg7 7. e3 0–0 8. Nge2 Nc6 9. 0–0 b6 10. b3 Ba6 11. Ba3

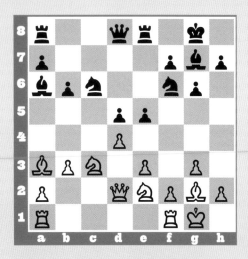

13. dxe5 Nxe5 14. Rfd1
Byrne wants to relieve the pin on his e2 knight. But 14. Rad1 would have been better.

14. ... Nd3! 15. Qc2?

The opening stage is equal.

11. ... Re8 12. Qd2 e5!

Fischer accepts the isolation of his d-pawn, seeing that he will have compensating activity for his pieces. Interestingly, modern-day computers confirm his legendary chess instincts by choosing this as the best move.

15. Nf4 Ne4 16. Nxe4 dxe4 17. Rab1 Rc8 is objectively better, but Black would have a dominating game with his outpost on d3.

15. ... Nxf2!
"The key to Black's previous play. The complete justification for this sac does not become apparent until White resigns!"—Fischer.

**16. Kxf2 Ng4+ 17. Kg1 Nxe3
18. Qd2**

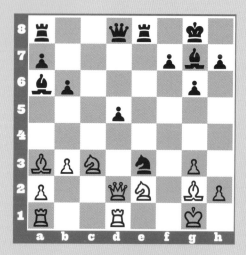

Byrne still thought Fischer was lost here. The grandmaster commentators in the next room thought so as well. But then came ...

18. ... Nxg2!!

"This dazzling move came as the shocker ... the culminating combination is of such depth that, even at the very moment at which I resigned, both grandmasters who were commenting on the play for the spectators in a separate room believed I had a won game!"— Robert Byrne.

19. Kxg2 d4! 20. Nxd4 Bb7+
"The king is at Black's mercy."— Fischer

21. Kf1
The grandmasters were still telling an excited crowd that Bobby Fischer was lost.

21. ... Qd7! White resigns

The commentators were bewildered. Fischer lamented: "A bitter disappointment. I'd hoped for 22. Qf2 Qh3+ 23. Kg1 Re1+!! 24. Rxe1 Bxd4 with mate to follow shortly." Fischer's intended *coup de grace*, 24. ... Bxd4, is an example of deflection. To avoid capture, the white queen would have to take the black bishop, allowing 25. ... Qg2#.

66 If your opponent is of choleric temper, seek to irritate him. Pretend to be weak, that he may grow arrogant. 99

Rope-a-dope of the chessboard

In Michal Krasenkow v Hikaru Nakamura, Black wins by giving his opponent the opportunity to play what appears to be a withering combination. White even gets to capture a piece while discovering an attack on Black's queen—but this irresistible plan rebounds as Black has foreseen an explosive counter. Truly the rope-a-dope of the chessboard!

We're now up to truly modern times. Although strategic and defensive techniques have strengthened dramatically over the decades, this game proves that it is still possible to land a deadly bomb that the opponent never sees coming. Out of an ordinary position, the daring Nakamura, now four-time US Champion and one of the world's top five players, conjures up a plan that draws his opponent into making a game-losing decision.

None of our Model Campaigns features weak opposition. Nakamura's opponent, Krasenkow, is a leading grandmaster and one of the strongest Polish players since World War II, with many best-game awards of his own.

MICHAL KRASENKOW (POLAND) v
HIKARU NAKAMURA (USA)
CASINO DE BARCELONA, 2007

1. Nf3 Nf6 2. c4
The game has transposed into an
English Opening.

**2. .. e6 3. g3 d5 4. Bg2 Be7
5. 0–0 0–0 6. b3 a5 7. Nc3 c6
8. d4 Nbd7 9. Qc2 b6 10. e4**

Although White at first ignored the
center, he's now given it a full-on
blitz.

10. ... Ba6
Black defends indirectly from the
flanks with this pin on the c4 pawn.

**11. Nd2 c5 12. exd5 cxd4
13. Nb5 exd5 14. Nxd4 Rc8**

The game is equal. Now, if he had
seen what was coming, White would
have played 15. a4.

**15. Re1 b5 16. Bb2 Re8 17. Qd1
bxc4 18. bxc4 Qb6 19. Rb1
dxc4 20. Nc6**

Setting up a discovery on Black's
queen, which Nakamura fearlessly
permits!

20. ... Rxc6 21. Bxf6

21. ... Qxf2+!!
But this bolt-from-the-blue queen sacrifice wins by force!

22. Kxf2
There's no future in not accepting the sacrifice: 22. Kh1 Qxf6 23. Bxc6 Qxc6+ leaves Black materially ahead and White's king open to attack.

22. ... Bc5+ 23. Kf3
If 23. Kf1 c3+ (discovered check) 24. Re2 c2 (double attack and decoy) 25. Qxc2 Bxe2+ 26. Ke1 Bd3+ (discovered check), winning the queen.

23. ... Rxf6+ 24. Kg4

White's king is caught in a mating net. White is ahead in material, but his big guns are out of the action while his leader is on dangerous ground.

24. ...Ne5+ 25. Kg5
If instead 25. Rxe5, then Nakamura foresaw 25. ... Bc8+! 26. Kh4 Rxe5, with play similar to the game.

25. ... Rg6+ 26. Kh5 f6 27. Rxe5 Rxe5+ 28. Kh4 Bc8 White resigns

White resigns in the face of certain death. Dealing with the threat of ... Rh6# costs too much. If 29. g4 Bf2+ 30. Kh3 Rh6#.

> **66** Therefore the skillful leader subdues the enemy's troops without any fighting; he captures their cities without laying siege to them; he overthrows their kingdom without lengthy operations in the field. **99**

"Magnus style"

A game in "Magnus style" means no long opening innovations, no early complications. He simply outplays his opponent strategically and then crashes through with a few neat tactics.

Magnus Carlsen became a grandmaster at 13 and 10 years later won the World Championship. His style is a bit different from many of his colleagues. He doesn't come to the board displaying a lot of home-cooked opening surprises.

In this game, his opponent once shared the World Championship title and was still at the top of his game. Veselin Topalov is known for producing tactical complications—"fire on the board." But this time, he simply isn't given the opportunity.

MAGNUS CARLSEN (NORWAY) v
VESELIN TOPALOV (BULGARIA)
NANJING, CHINA, 2010

1. e4 e5 2. Nf3 Nc6 3. Bb5 a6
The Ruy Lopez—and the response for
Black that Paul Morphy favored 150
years before.

4. Ba4 Nf6 5. 0–0 Be7 6. d3!?

Carlsen postpones d4 in order to
choose his setup according to
Black's choices.

**6. ... b5 7. Bb3 d6 8. a4 Rb8 9.
axb5 axb5 10. Nbd2**
Normally White would play 10. Nc3.
But Carlsen's move is not bad and
puts both players on their own
resources.

10. ... 0–0 11. Re1 Bd7
12. c3 Ra8 13. Rxa8 Qxa8
14. d4

Carlsen chooses this moment to
thrust in the center. The game is
equal but difficult to play for both
sides.

14. ... h6 15. Nf1

In the Ruy Lopez, it's typical to see
White bringing his queenside knight
to the kingside, where White hopes
to attack.

15. ... Re8 16. Ng3 Qc8 17. Nh4

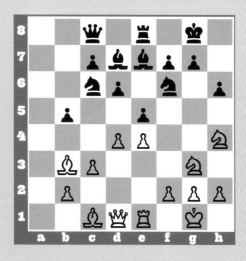

Carlsen starts his fight for the initiative. His knights are eyeing f5 as a staging point for an attack against Black's king.

17. ... Bf8?!

An inaccuracy. Black relinquishes the bishop pair for no genuine compensation. Instead, 17. ... Na5 would lead to complications not unfavorable for Black.

18. Ng6!

Of course, the knight is immune to capture because the pawn on f7 is pinned by White's bishop on b3.

18. ... Na5 19. Nxf8 Rxf8

If instead 19. ... Nxb3 20. Nxd7 Qxd7 (or 20 .... Nxc1 21.Nxf6+ gxf6 22. Nf5 and the threat of 23. Qg4+ and 24. Qg7 mate is devastating) 21. Qxb3. White is a piece up.

20. Bc2 Re8 21. f4!

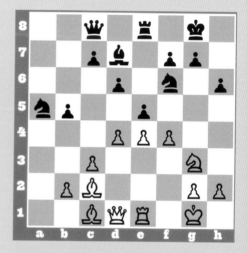

Carlsen believes in his big center and bishop pair, which is aimed at the enemy kingside.

21. ... Bg4 22. Qd3 exf4?
Sitting tight with 22. ... Qb8 would make a tougher defense.

23. Bxf4 Nc4 24. Bc1!
A controlled retreat. Black is helpless now.

24. ... c5 25. Rf1 cxd4 26. cxd4 Qd8 27. h3 Be6 28. b3 Qa5 29. Kh2

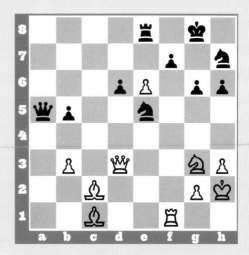

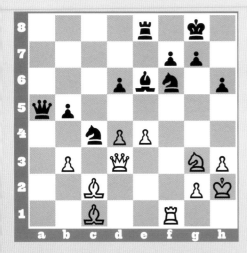

Carlsen sees no need to make things complicated. No "fire on the board" for Topalov this time! It's true that 29. bxc4 Bxc4 30. Qd2 Qxd2 31. Bxd2 Bxf1 32. Kxf1 is probably won for White, but it's complex and leaves a lot of game to play before victory. With his last move, Carlsen sidesteps the complications and instead prepares the final assault.

29. ... Nh7 30. e5 g6
To stop Qxh7+.

31. d5
White's center pawns are rolling forward, demolishing the defense. Carlsen has a final neat trick up his sleeve.

31. ... Nxe5 32. dxe6! Black resigns

Black knows he's helpless against Carlsen's attack. Let's see why. If Black captures the queen with 32. ... Nxd3, there follows 33. exf7+ Kf8 34. Bxh6+ Ke7 35. fxe8Q+ Kxe8 36. Bxd3 and not only does Black lose the g-pawn, but also the knight. For example, 36. ... Qc7 37. Bxg6+ Kd8 38. Rf7.

Analysis diagram after 38. Rf7

White's material advantage is overwhelming.

Other books by Al Lawrence

With Grandmaster Lev Alburt:
Chess for the Gifted and Busy
Chess Rules of Thumb
Three Days with Bobby Fischer
Chess Training Pocket Book II

With Jim Eade:
The Chess Player's Bible

Chess on the Internet

www.uschess.org
The home of the United States Chess Federation, offering free chess news and lots of other information. Find clubs and tournaments close to your home.
www.fide.com

The homepage of the International Chess Federation, with nearly 160 member countries.
www.chess.com

Play others from all over the world and get an online rating for free. Pay a reasonable premium to add high-quality instructional resources, including videos and puzzles.
www.chesskid.com

The kids-oriented branch of chess.com.
www.chessbase.com

International chess news and instructive articles.

Reading list

A single, condensed volume that can take you from the end of this book to tournament-tough expertise is *Chess for the Gifted and Busy* by three-time US Champion Grandmaster Lev Alburt and Al Lawrence. Lev Alburt's *Comprehensive Chess Course* is a multi-volume set written with Roman Pelts and other high-powered co-authors. Each volume provides extensive instruction on different phases of the game. These books are explained and are available at www.chesswithlev.com. Or write to Grandmaster Lev Alburt at P.O. Box 534, Gracie Square Station, New York, NY 10028.

The Chess Player's Bible by Jim Eade and Al Lawrence is a single-volume encyclopedia of chess-playing wisdom.

Jeremy Silman is another chess author whose books are always especially instructive and well-written.

Authors' acknowledgments

"*The Art of War* is an immense study which comprises all others."
Napoleon, Emperor of Europe

"Chess is war over the board."
Bobby Fischer, Emperor of the Chessboard

Our thanks to Kate Kirby and the crew of Quarto Publishing for the idea of this book and their confidence in our ability to bring it to fruition. Two chess players trying to get a book just right are a lot to put up with. Our skillful overseas editor, Claire Waite Brown, displayed the patience and ingenuity of a chessmaster. At home, we must credit Mary Lawrence and Woman International Grandmaster Sabina Foisor for both their encouragement and their tireless double-checking. We promise never again to ask, "Is this version a little clearer?"—until the next book.

Al Lawrence
International Grandmaster Elshan Moradiabadi

Credits

18percentgrey, Shutterstock.com, pp.82, 145
Zhuda, Shutterstock.com, p.12
Arzawen, Shutterstock.com, p.136
BestPhotoStudio, Shutterstock.com, p.93
Bildagentur Zoonar GmbH, Shutterstock.com, p.90
BortN66, Shutterstock.com, p.65
Chendongshan, Shutterstock.com, p.67
Collins, Judith, Alamy Stock Photo, p.42
Corbis, pp.16, 18, 26, 54, 62, 68, 98
DWD-photo, Alamy Stock Photo, p.74
Dziobek, Shutterstock.com, p.102
Xiaofeng, Yang, Shutterstock.com, p.124
Elwell, Christopher, p.112
Feawt, Shutterstock.com, p.86
Hung Chung Chih, Shutterstock.com, p.130
Kholoet, Arthiti, Shutterstock.com, p.23
Kuryatov, Georgy, Shutterstock.com, p.58
LongkauD, Shutterstock.com, pp.2, 22, 111
Luxorphoto, Shutterstock.com, pp.77, 138
Manczurov, Shutterstock.com, p.34, 88
MJTH, Shutterstock.com, p.24
Pavelgr, Shutterstock.com, p.4
PhotosIndia.com LLC, Alamy Stock Photo, p.142
Pryzmat, Shutterstock.com, pp.20, 147
Samokhin, Roman, p.72
Saunders, Gordon, Shutterstock.com, pp.63, 80, 154
Sobko, Dima, Shutterstock.com, p.60
Soon, Patricia, Shutterstock.com, p.151
TonyV3112, Shutterstock.com, p.84
Trinset, Shutterstock.com, p.94
Valentina Photos, Shutterstock.com, p.48
Vrublevski, Denis, Shutterstock.com, pp.31, 44
Vugenfirer, Yan, Shutterstock.com, p.53
Yanugkelid, Shutterstock.com, p.120
Couper, Harley, Shutterstock.com, p.38
Eky Studio, Shutterstock.com, p.105